Dorte Nielsen & Sarah Thurber

The secret of the highly creative thinker

How to make connections others don't

BIS Publishers

BIS Publishers
Building Het Sieraad
Postjesweg 1
1057 DT Amsterdam
The Netherlands
T +31 (0)20 515 02 30
bis@bispublishers.com
www.bispublishers.com

ISBN 978 90 6369 415 9

Design: Dorte Nielsen and Katrine Granholm
Typographic consultant: Henrik Birkvig
Cover design: Katrine Granholm and Ulrik Jessen
Illustrations: Andrew Smart
Set in Gotham and Eames Century Modern

Most of the photos in this book are student work from the Creative
Communications department at the Danish School of Media and Journalism.
A full list of credits appears at the back of the book.

www.see-connections.com

Contents

Foreword

Creativity has moved up in the world. Where it used to be a nice to have, now it's a need to have.

Today, educators consider it among the highest form of learning. Psychologists consider it among the highest forms of self-actualization. Business executives consider it among the most critical characteristics of modern leadership. Frankly, creativity is not a luxury. It is a 21st century survival skill. Professional and personal success depend on it.

There has never been a more important time to cultivate creative thinking in our students, our citizens, our employees and ourselves. While creativity sometimes seems magical, in fact, as authors Dorte Nielsen and Sarah Thurber point out, creative thinking has its own distinct patterns, guidelines and mechanics, which when we understand them, can support better thinking, better collaboration and better solutions.

Our fast moving world demands creative responses, and the practical strategies and exercises in this book promote exactly that: creativity on demand. Why wait for the muse? Learn to take responsibility for your own creativity. Nielsen and Thurber offer proven practices that help you to do just that. Commit to these methods and you will be able to produce breakthrough ideas whenever and wherever you wish.

I'm delighted to see this book reach readers everywhere.

Gerard J. Puccio, PhD
Director, International Center for Studies in Creativity
New York

"Highly creative people are good at seeing connections.

By enhancing your ability to see connections, you can enhance your creativity."

Dorte Nielsen

Introduction

It all began at an ad agency in London. It was the early 1990s—a golden age in advertising—and I was in the thick of it, working as an art director in the creative department in one of the largest ad agencies in the world. Things were good. With awards rolling in and accolades mounting, I got an invitation from my old school, the Graphic Arts Institute of Denmark, to run a series of guest lectures on creativity and creative thinking.

Colleagues scoffed at the notion of teaching creativity. "You've either got it or you don't," they said. Some closest to me warned that I was wasting my time and squandering my career trying to teach creativity to others. But my students' earnest desire to learn compelled me to try. Like many before me, I began to ponder the question "How can you teach people to become more creative?"

I became a stealthy observer. At the agency, I watched creative professionals hatch ideas and build award-winning campaigns. At the Institute, I watched students battle to produce original work. Over time, I noticed a striking pattern. It all seemed to boil down to just one thing.

People who are good at having ideas are good at seeing connections.

Could it really be this simple? Could teaching people to see connections be a way to help them be more creative?

The idea was a little unorthodox. Most creativity training focused on process and tools. Seeing connections is simply a skill—a teachable skill, one I suspected was fundamental to creative thinking. So I took a leap. I built a creativity curriculum on the cornerstone of seeing connections.

What started as a hunch developed into a series of exercises, which now form the backbone of a curriculum for highly creative thinkers.

Our school is now part of the Danish School of Media Journalism. Each year, around 500 aspiring art directors, copyrighters and conceptual thinkers apply to our department. We accept 24. Our graduates get job offers from premier agencies in New York, London, Paris, Sao Paulo and Shanghai.

If international awards are any measure, this new approach to teaching creativity worked. Today the Creative Communication education I founded back in 2007 wins more advertising awards than any other public bachelors degree program in the world. Our students are collecting international awards for creativity at D&AD, Cannes Lions, Epica, CREAM and Eurobest, among others. Of course, all of the credit goes to the students, but I think they would agree that their hard work and dedication coupled with these bold new training methods have enhanced their native creativity.

Over the years, I have found there's a need for a book on creativity that goes beyond the teaching of creative process and tools, and also gives you a practical approach for how to enhance your innate ability to think creatively.

So I contacted my wonderful friend and creativity partner Sarah Thurber, managing partner of the FourSight company in Chicago. She, too, has devoted 20 years of her career to teaching and writing about creativity. During our graduate studies together (in pursuit of a Master of Science in Creativity at the International Center for Studies in Creativity in New York), we discovered the power of our combined expertise in advertising, writing, publishing, researching and teaching creativity. It's our aim to create a unique book that combines a very hands-on and practical approach to creativity with a solid scholarly foundation.

We see this book as an opportunity to dispel the myth that creative talent is something possessed by a gifted minority. This is our chance to pass on the secret of highly creative people to a much wider audience and share the knowledge, techniques and training that people need to enhance their own innate creativity.

Dorte Nielsen

"People say: You can't teach creativity.

Then again, creativity is all about reversing assumptions."

Sarah Thurber

Part One

The nature of seeing connections

Discover the secret of the highly creative thinker. Take an inside look at how to see and make new connections that lead to unexpected and original products, from simple, everyday solutions to great scientific breakthroughs.

Lampella by Neela Menik Wedage

The secret of the highly creative thinker

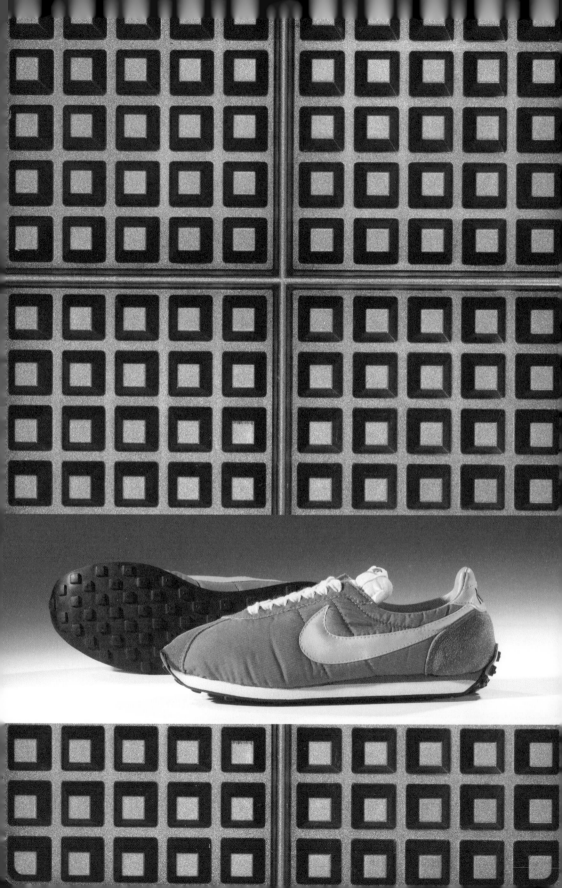

The core of creative thinking

One summer morning in the early 1970s, Bill and Barbara Bowerman were fixing waffles for breakfast. Bill, the head running coach at the University of Oregon, was bemoaning the fact that his runners didn't have track shoes that could grip the new artificial turf.

Having coached thirty-three Olympians, he was always on the lookout for better athletic gear. In the 1960s, he had co-launched a company to import light-weight running shoes from Japan. He even had a lab in his house where he could experiment.

Now he was looking for a lighter, faster shoe, one without spikes that could still grip the new running track.

At that moment, Barbara pulled a waffle off the hot waffle iron. Staring at the waffle, Bill suddenly made a connection. The grid pattern on the waffle might just create the perfect grip for the sole of a running shoe. He grabbed the waffle iron and ran to his lab.

By the end of the day, he had prototyped the shoe that would earn him his first patent and launch his company to international fame: The Nike Waffle Trainer.

The story is a perfect example of what happens at the moment a creative idea is conceived.

Coach Bowerman had been puzzling over his challenge for weeks when an unexpected connection at the breakfast table unlocked it. In an instant, the DNA of the waffle and the DNA of the running shoe combined in his mind to bring something entirely new into being.

Creativity is just that: the ability to bring new and valuable things into being. You can cultivate that ability. We'd like to teach you how.

This book serves up the findings of seventy years of research into the science of creativity and sets you on a path to pursue your individual creative potential. While most teachers aim to teach you things they know, our aim is to teach you how to come up with things nobody knows, things that you invent.

Everyone may be born with a different level of creativity, but everybody can learn skills that help creative thinking along. Making connections is such a skill. In fact it's an essential skill.

Making connections helps you see new options, create unusual solutions, and make the far-fetched combinations that lead to original ideas. Training your ability to see and make connections helps you build mental flexibility, agility, and adaptability. It also helps you come up with original ideas, which is a hallmark of creative thinkers. The truth about creative thinking is

People who are good at having creative ideas are good at seeing connections.

By training your ability to see connections, you improve your capacity to think creatively.

So we're going to help you crank up your connection-making machinery. First, we'll talk about the nature of connections. Then we'll share the research on how highly creative people think. We'll tell you what the neuroscientists have to say and walk you through a short course on creative thinking.

Finally we'll enroll you in our creative connections boot camp and take you through a series of exercises and tools that will sharpen your creative reflexes and build your creative confidence.

Like playing scales for musicians or running laps for athletes, seeing connections is a foundational skill for creative thinkers. Highly creative people have it as their default setting. Don't worry if you don't. Just like physical conditioning, these exercises will help make your mental muscles stronger, and allow you to see connections you couldn't see before.

At Christmastime in Denmark, Dorte's family lights an advent candle.
She blew the flame out when she saw a connection between the wick
and the Christmas countdown.

6
7
8
9
10
11
12
13
14
15

The moment of conception happens when two unlike items connect.
Tammes Bernstein saw this connection happening at the breakfast table.

There's an old Chinese proverb: "When the winds of change blow, some build walls, others build windmills." In periods of change, our natural instinct is to dig in and build walls that shield us.

Creativity is what helps us build windmills. It's the type of thinking that helps us adventure into unfamiliar territory, see opportunities, generate options, and come up with new solutions in our private lives, our politics, our schools and our work. In business, creativity fuels innovation. There is no innovation without creativity.

Creativity used to be a bonus, an extra, a perk, or just a polite way to say you're a bit odd. "That's so creative, dear." But as technology and global competition cut into our jobs and market share, creative thinking skills are looking less like a luxury and more like a necessity.

Recently, IBM undertook the largest ever survey of CEOs, talking to more than fifteen hundred organizational leaders in thirty-three countries. CEOs reported that their most pressing concern was coping with the increasing rate of change. No surprise. What caught media attention was the leadership quality they voted as being the most important: creativity. Creativity is their best hope for adapting to change, for building windmills.

They weren't talking about artistic expression, which is one form of creativity, but about creative problem solving, the type of thinking that allows you to remain open to ambiguity, see gaps, follow hunches, reverse assumptions, spot strategic opportunities, connect ideas, and imagine a future so compelling that others will follow your lead.

Today creative thinking is becoming a necessity in every job. A new study from Oxford predicted the future impact of technology on nearly seven hundred jobs. The analysis showed that computers will be taking over any job that doesn't require a personal touch. That means that just to hold a job, everyone will rely on their creative intelligence— their ability to think flexibly and deliver solutions outside of standard operating procedures.

A new study from Adobe showed that, compared to other job skills, problem solving and creativity have gained the most value in driving salary increases in the last five years.

In this book we will help you boost your ability to innovate and think creatively. We will teach you to make connections that others don't.

"When the winds of change blow, some build walls other build windmills."

Old Chinese proverb

Lightbulb by Trine Quistgaard

The unexpected connection

Once you start looking, you'll find connections everywhere. Free association, comparisons, gap finding and cross-fertilization are all forms of connection making. During incubation, when you are pondering over a challenge, your mind is simply waiting to make a connection between a trigger and your challenge. And it doesn't matter if the idea trigger is a newspaper headline, a waffle iron, or a lady on the bus with a funny hat. The point is, you have made a connection. Making connections is at the core of every creative process.

The more unexpected the connection, the more dramatic the breakthrough. Greek philosopher Heraclitus was onto this more than two thousand years ago when he said, "The unexpected connection is more powerful than one that is obvious." Consider the example of Johannes Gutenberg's printing press. Gutenberg was an entrepreneur and inventor by nature and a goldsmith by trade. He had already invented a movable, metal set of type, but he spent years struggling to find an effective way to transfer ink to the paper. The print impressions he could make using the more standard approaches of rubbing or stamping rendered poor quality text. One day, on a trip to a local winery, he noticed the screw mechanism on a wine press. In a flash, he saw a new way to transfer ink from his moveable type to the page. As with many great insights, the connection Gutenberg made between the wine press and the printing press seems simple, almost obvious to us now. But in the 15th century it was unexpected, and became the light that ushered Europe out of the Dark Ages.

There are plenty of other famous examples of unexpected creative connections: Isaac Newton connected a falling apple with the force of gravity. Gandhi connected nonviolence to revolutions. Coco Chanel connected suits to pearls. Elvis connected African-American blues to white teenage girls. In these and countless other cases, a creative connection resulted in something larger than the sum of its parts. The equation 1+1=3 may not work in math, but it's a perfect description of what happens when your mind makes a new and valuable connection.

Twist Cone by Mads Schmidt

Connections are everywhere

Thanks to Mikkel Møller's visual connection, we finally have a Christmas tree that looks like the one we all drew in primary school.

How highly creative people think

Sit back and watch a highly creative person think. Just watch. "Let's colonize Mars." "Your sandwich looks like it has a moustache."

Creative people are forever surprising us by challenging assumptions, flipping ideas, and expanding, contracting, and recombining things in their heads. It's a three-ring circus in there.

Actually, that's not a bad analogy. While less creative people seem to think in logical, linear patterns, highly creative people think in analogical, web-like patterns—connecting all sorts of things that more conventional thinkers wouldn't ever put together. What looks like ADHD to you, may well be creative genius at work.

In creative departments of advertising agencies, creative professionals will spend the day waltzing through a wide range of topics, pulling ideas out of thin air, making connections left and right and spring-boarding from data to inspiration. They are jugglers, throwing around high speed, high quality, original ideas that somehow still manage to stay relevant and aloft, whether the focus of the day is hair care or helicopters. For better or for worse, creative people seem to have the ability to look at the same thing as everyone else, and see something completely different.

What highly creative people do can seem magical, or completely off-the-wall. Who could have predicted that a cartoon mouse would become an international icon of creativity? That a cell phone could be the object of one's affection? Or that electric cars could be sexy? But there is a method to the madness.

Highly creative people make connections all the time. Making a connection is like having a mini "Aha!" moment. It has the same quality of discovery and surprise. Aha moments happen every day to nearly everyone. They are often simple insights. They may not be flashy to anyone else, but if it's new and useful to you, it qualifies as a connection.

*When others see a bike
Picasso sees a bull*

Managua, Nicaragua by Elliott Erwitt

Visual connections

When most of us look at a bike, we see a bike. When Picasso looked at a bike, he saw a bull. He described the famous sculpture he made of a bicycle seat with handlebar horns, saying,

"Guess how I made the bull's head? One day, in a pile of objects all jumbled up together, I found an old bicycle seat right next to a rusty set of handlebars. In a flash, they joined together in my head. The idea of the Bull's Head came to me before I had a chance to think. All I did was weld them together."

It takes a creative thinker to recognize a connection that is hiding in plain sight. Elliott Erwitt, who photographed Marylin Monroe, Che Guevara, and Jackie Kennedy, also photographed the old woman sitting behind the gourds on the opposite page. He said,

"To me, photography is an art of observation. It's about finding something interesting in an ordinary place... I've found it has little to do with the things you see and everything to do with the way you see them."

Verbal connections

Making connections is by no means limited to the visual arts. Literature is chock full of connections. For centuries, writers, poets, rappers and politicians have been using similes and metaphors to woo, rant, entertain, persuade, teach and rule. Writers are masters at illuminating one thing by connecting it to another.

"My love is like a red, red rose," wrote poet Robert Burns. Of course, we all know his love is not a rose. His love is a feeling, and a rose is a flower. The language doesn't work on a literal level. The mismatch of the words "love" and "rose" creates a verbal vacuum that forces our imagination to fill in the gap. We automatically conjure up the character traits these two items might share. We imagine that like the rose, his love is alive, blooming, beautiful, delicate, arresting, and red hot.

Analogies are more complex than similes and metaphors. They ask us to connect many things at once. Fictional character Forrest Gump offered surprising wisdom with his innocent analogy: "Life is like a box of chocolates. You never know what you're going to get."

"If you look at history, innovation doesn't come just from giving people incentives; it comes from creating environments where their ideas can connect."

Steven Johnson

World-class connections

World-class creative accomplishments are often the result of not one, but thousands of connections and mini "aha moments," each built upon the one before.

Mozart started composing music when he was five. Today we think of him as a musical genius, but his early works were largely derivative and unremarkable. "People err who think my art comes easily to me," he said. "I assure you, dear friend, nobody has devoted so much time and thought to compositions as I."

Mozart built on the work of Bach, Hayden and Handel. Every piece he wrote was an opportunity to explore a new musical connection. Mozart wrote over six hundred compositions. Before he died at age 35, he was, indeed, a musical genius.

Picasso, too, started his career, producing early works that could easily have been mistaken for other painters of the day. He studied the great masters as well as his contemporaries. Over seven decades, Picasso produced nearly fifty thousand pieces of art. Each allowed him to explore a different visual connection. His master works changed the way we see the world.

Scientific connections

Scientists are among the most deliberate connection-makers of all. They know that scientific discovery is almost never the result of a single connection, but a series of connections, each one standing on the shoulders of the one before.

Thomas Edison knew the value of making connections. He understood that finding the right connection was the key to invention. Many of his inventions didn't work. He wasn't concerned. He said, "I make more mistakes than anyone else I know. And, sooner or later, I patent most of them." He patented cement houses and electric voting machines and photographs and electric car batteries. Through out the 20th century he held the world record for number of patents. In fact, he was just as committed to ruling out connections that didn't work as he was to finding connections that did. After testing a thousand or more filaments for his light bulb, he famously stated, "Results! Why, man, I have gotten a lot of results. I know several thousand things that don't work."

Connections Hall of Fame

If there were such a thing as the "Connections Hall of Fame," George de Mestral, the inventor of Velcro®, would be in it.

The legendary tale goes that in 1948, Mestral was hiking with his dog in the hills of Switzerland and returned home to find both the animal and himself covered with burrs from the trail. His struggle to remove the burrs piqued his curiosity.

He put the burrs under a microscope for a closer look and discovered the tiny hooks at their tips. Mestral saw the connection between the burrs' hooks and the possibility of creating a synthetic fastening system.

It's a classic story of connection making, but did you know that even the name Velcro is a connection? It connects the words "velour," the smooth fabric on one side of the fastener and "crochet," the pokey crochet-like hooks on the other. Vel + Cro = Velcro.

Biomimicry

Inspired in part by the Velcro story, today, scientists, engineers, and inventors, are now intentionally looking to nature for clues, solutions, analogies and insights. They call the practice "Biomimicry." Nature, they argue, boasts 3.8 billion years of experience in product design, recycling, sustainability, and complex systems. Why not look there for inspiration and new connections?

Indeed, the water repellent properties of lotus leaves have helped engineers develop self-cleaning glass. The communal activity of beehives helped business consultants understand organizational behavior. And a bird beak recently saved Japan's bullet train.

The story goes that when Japanese engineers proudly unveiled the latest model of the bullet train, they didn't anticipate the downside of speed. The new train came zooming out of tunnels so fast that it created

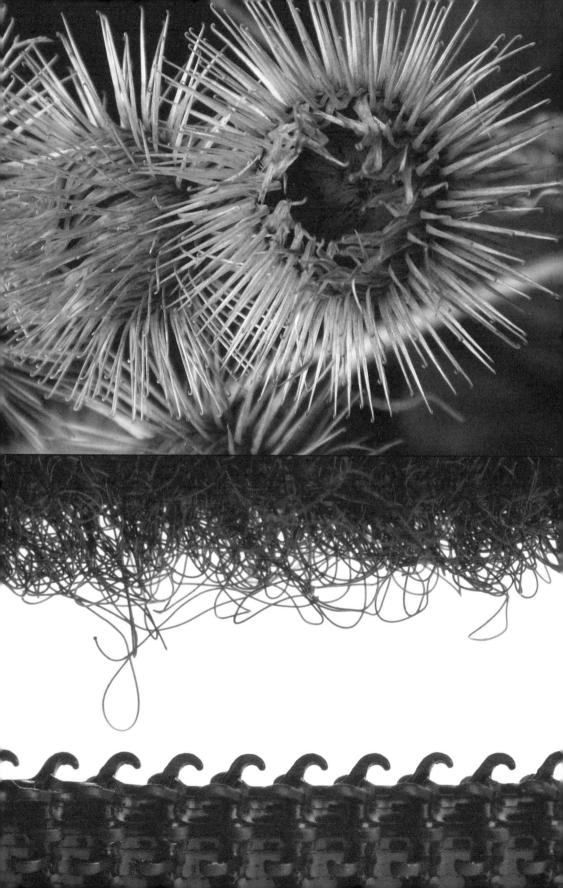

a sonic boom. Neighbors from half a kilometer away complained. The sound was clearly out of regulation, putting the new train at risk of being decommissioned.

Company engineer Eiji Nakatsu studied the problem. He recognized that the sound came from the train emerging from the tunnel and hitting the higher air pressure outside. He went in search of an analogy that would help him study something that moved seamlessly at high speed from a low pressure environment into a high pressure one.

Nakatsu was also a birdwatcher, who knew that a kingfisher could enter the water without creating a ripple. The long wedged shape of its beak allowed it to move seamlessly from air to water. He redesigned the front of the train to mimic the kingfisher's beak. The connection he made not only resolved the noise problem, it let the train use fifteen percent less electricity and travel ten percent faster.

Scientific inventor Louis Pasteur said, "Chance favors the prepared mind." Connections do too. Many of the creative connections described in this chapter follow a similar pattern. People who saw connections had already devoted intense time and energy in the direction of their creative breakthrough.

Bowerman was obsessed with finding a running shoe that would grip the track. Gutenberg was determined to find a better way to transfer ink to paper. Edison hired an army of inventors to help him find a filament that could keep the light bulb burning. All of these creators were alight with curiosity, experience, intelligence, persistence, and a perceived need. But ultimately, it was their ability to make an unexpected connection that catalyzed their creative breakthrough.

As Edison said, "Nearly every man who develops an idea works it up to the point where it looks impossible, and then he gets discouraged. That's not the place to become discouraged." That's the place to start looking for a connection.

Part Two

The theories
behind it all

*Does creativity really boil down to
connection making? Meet thinkers from the
1930s, researchers from the 1960s, and
neuroscientists today who think it does. Take
the world's fastest course on creative thinking.*

*If you simply can't wait another minute
to do the exercises, skip to Part 3, and
read this later.*

Tie by Maria Birkholm Marcher

The research on making connections

"Creativity is just connecting things."

Steve Jobs

The theoretical foundation

We aren't the first to make the link between connection making and creativity.

In 1939, advertising executive James Webb Young wrote a book titled *A Technique for Producing Ideas.* "An idea is nothing more nor less than a new combination of old elements," he wrote. "The capacity to bring old elements into new combinations depends largely on the ability to see relationships."

In 1945, Albert Einstein wrote a letter trying to explain his own mental process as a scientist. He described his mechanism of creative thinking as "rather vague play" with images and symbols that he could reproduce and combine. In fact, he wrote, "This combinatory play seems to be the essential feature in productive thought."

In 1950, Australian animal pathologist W.I.B. Beveridge wrote a book for researchers called *The Art of Scientific Investigation,* in which he described the nature of scientific breakthrough. He wrote, "Originality often consists in linking up ideas whose connection was not previously suspected."

Connection making really blossomed in the 1960s, when researchers, writers, scientists, social activists, and business people all seemed to independently come to the conclusion that making connections was at the core of the creative process.

Popular American folksinger Pete Seeger, who dropped out of Harvard University to pursue a life of social activism, said, "In solving a problem, you often have to make connections between two things that aren't usually connected." He galvanized a generation of political activists when he connected the song "We Shall Overcome" to the Civil Rights movement. About his own songwriting, he acknowledged that creating something new was often an act of recombining words and musical scales that had been around for centuries.

Synectics

While musicians were connecting songs to social activism, creativity researchers and consultants George Prince and William Gordon recognized the value of connection making in business. Early in their careers, they joined the invention design group at Arthur D. Little to conduct creativity experiments. They pioneered the use of video cameras to record collaborative brainstorming sessions. They scrutinized hours of tapes, looking for patterns that could reveal how groups arrived at creative insights.

They discovered that part of what allowed groups to make new, valuable connections was their ability to break the existing connections they had with current norms, assumptions and expectations. As in quantum science, Prince said, "all newness comes from chaos, where everything is disconnected and random and new connections can happen." But who would hire creative consultants who purposely created chaos in a business meeting?

It was Gordon who struck on the solution. They would use analogies to create mental excursions that would draw people out of their habitual thinking patterns and take them on a mental exploration "to make the strange familiar and the familiar strange." Prince explained: "Using excursions, we were creating a 'safe' chaos." They called the new problem-solving approach "Synectics," from the Greek, meaning the joining together of different and apparently irrelevant elements.

The Synectics approach is powered by making and breaking connections. A Synectics expert might help packaging designers solve the problem of potato chip breakage by asking, "How is a potato chip like a leaf?" Or challenge a psychiatrist to consider, "How is a personality like a snowflake?" Or prompt a computer programmer to seek insights by imagining, "How is the Internet like a plumbing system for information?" In each case, the mind, bumped out of familiar territory, begins to seek new connections and come up with new ideas.

The Remote Associates Test

While connection making was alive in 1960s street protests and business boardrooms, it was also alive in ivory towers. In the psychology department at the University of Michigan, researchers Sarnoff and Martha Mednick were busy testing an entirely new theory of creativity, one based on making connections or what they called "associations." They defined creative thinking as "the forming of associative elements into new combinations which either meet specified requirements or are in some way useful." Through rigorous research, the Mednicks found that highly creative people have richer associative lives than less creative people. In 1967, Sarnoff Mednick described his research findings about highly creative people: "They can produce a greater number of associations to a wide variety of stimuli. They also show associative endurance; their rate of idea production does not drop off as rapidly as it does for the less creative individual. In addition, their ideas are unusual, and are less dominated by a single track. Furthermore, their associations are likely to vary from occasion to occasion."

The Mednicks' theory of creativity took the operational form of the Remote Associates Test, fondly known as the RAT. The test asks you to find a single word that makes sense when you combine it with each of 3 given words. For example, given the words FOUNTAIN, BAKING, and POP, you might think of the word SODA, because, by adding "soda" before or after the other words, you get soda fountain, baking soda, and soda pop. The Mednicks believed creative people would have an easier time making these remote associations, and therefore score higher.

Their theory and research broke new ground. However, as a test of creative ability, the RAT only worked part way. It works well at identifying creative individuals with high verbal IQs, but it altogether misses highly creative people who excel at visual or conceptual thinking. The RAT fell largely out of favor until recently when neuroscientists had to find a creativity test they could give to subjects lying stock-still in an MRI machine. Even so, it's a fun exercise in verbal connection making. You can try it yourself with the examples on the right.

Try the RAT

The Mednick's Remote Associates Test, the RAT, is based on word association. The task is to look at three given words and think of a fourth word that connects to each of the three. For example you could be given the three words:

Bird   Room   Tub

Your task is now to find a fourth word that connects to each of the words.

In this case the answer is "bath" because you can add the word bath to all three of the other words, as in birdbath, bathroom, and bathtub. Notice that the fourth word might either go in front or in back of each given word.

Now you try it:

Example 1:

Cottage   Swiss   Cake

Example 2:

Rocking   Wheel   High

Answer 1: Cheese. Answer 2: Chair.

"Associating seemingly disparate elements in new ways by finding a novel connection between them is the backbone of creativity."

Michael Michalko

"The Act of Creation"

In 1964, Nobel prizewinning writer, Arthur Koestler, wrote *The Act of Creation* in which he put forward an elaborate theory of human creativity. Building his case with countless examples of invention and discovery, he concluded that creativity is essentially an act of connection making. He called it "bisociation"—a putting together of two previously unrelated elements through a process of comparison, abstraction, and categorization.

To Koestler, analogies, metaphors, allegories, jokes, acting, identification and roleplaying were all forms of "bisociation," which he considered the cornerstone of creation.

IQ vs. The Torrance Test of Creative Thinking

Educational psychologist, E. Paul Torrance, published nearly two thousand works on creativity. He believed creativity should be taught in the classroom and argued that it was a type of intelligence overlooked by Alfred Binet's Intelligence Quotient (IQ) test. How could you measure originality with a test that sought only right answers? Such a test could never identify qualities of creative intelligence such as idea fluency, mental flexibility, originality and idea elaboration. So Torrance designed his own tests, and he awarded points for things like producing ideas, shifting perspectives and making novel connections. The test had not only verbal, but also visual and conceptual components.

Throughout the 1960s, Torrance gave his creativity tests to many schoolchildren and tracked the results over time. His research team revisited the students twenty-two, forty, and fifty years later. They discovered that IQ tests were actually poor predictors of creative achievement. Torrance's tests were three hundred percent more likely to predict the number of inventions, discoveries, and artistic accomplishments achieved in adulthood.

Torrance proved that the ability to get the right answer on an IQ test is no guarantee of a person's ability to produce new and useful work. The ability to think fluently, flexibly, and originally does.

If education strives to develop people who can innovate in business, science, sports, and the arts, he argued, we need to expand our view of intelligence and actively teach skills that promote creative thinking. Torrance believed that creativity training could literally change our minds. Forty years later, neuroscientists proved him right.

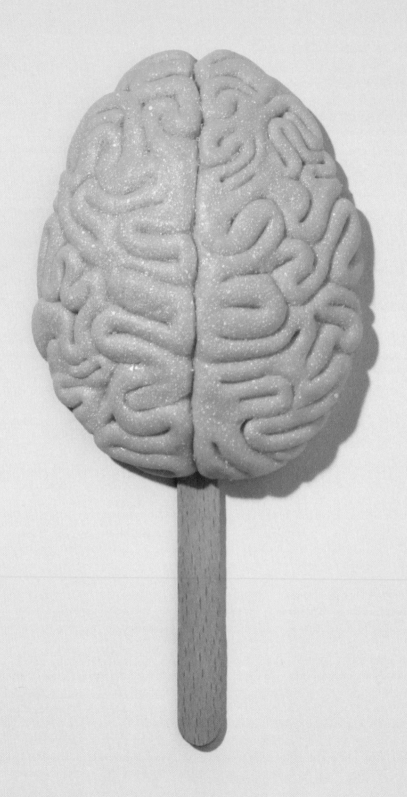

Brain Freeze by Jennifer Tonndorff

What the neuroscientists have to say

"The importance of association, and in particular, distant association, is confirmed by these studies."

Keith Sawyer

What neuroscientists have to say

Let's have a look inside your brain. What goes on when you're being creative? First of all, the whole thing lights up. Researchers have moved past the idea that creativity comes from just one part of your brain. "Creativity is not localized in one brain region," affirms creativity expert Keith Sawyer in his critical review of research on cognitive neuroscience. "Rather, creativity emerges from a complex network of neurons firing throughout the brain."

That means creativity is a whole-brain activity. But can scientists find a link between creativity and connection making?

In *Biological Bases of Creativity*, creativity researcher Colin Martindale says creative inspiration happens in a state of mind in which "attention is defocused, when thought is associative, and when a large number of mental representations are simultaneously activated." That is to say, creativity occurs in a mental state that's ripe for associative thinking—for seeing and making new connections. Sawyer, who surveyed a wide range of neuroscience studies, agrees: "The importance of association, and in particular, distant association, is confirmed by these studies."

So we're not just imagining that connection making is a key mechanism in creative thinking. But are creative people's brains actually different?

The brain of the creative thinker

Neurobiologist Andreas Fink offers insight. His research compares brain activity in highly creative and less creative individuals. The difference appears to be in the frontal lobe. Lower levels of cortical activation let highly creative people think more freely—as though their ideas let down their guard and fraternize with all the other ideas in their head. Creative thinkers are promiscuous connection makers. They naturally connect thoughts that others do not and generate ideas that can appear crazy, brilliant, chaotic, cool, unconventional, hilarious, ridiculous, odd, and original.

The brain of the conventional thinker

Conventional thinkers, by contrast, preserve mental boundaries that keep information neatly organized and tidily categorized. Their brains are a little more buttoned up. The information is kept in its proper place. The ideas don't tend to leap over. The ideas are appropriate. The information is accurate. These people might be world experts in their field, but when a well-meaning team member urges them to free associate, think outside the box or "brainstorm," nothing comes. For them brainstorming can seem like hell. New combinations and ideas are simply not as readily available to them. Their brains aren't wired to work that way. They have more mental constraints than highly creative thinkers.

Overcoming mental constraints

People have tried to overcome this limitation with various strategies. Australian inventors developed a thinking cap that runs electric current through the brain. English researchers claim that drinking a pint (or two) of beer will temporarily increase your creative quotient. Throughout history, writers, painters, poets, and creative geniuses of all kinds have experimented with everything from napping to narcotics. But the neuroscientists, seeking a more sustainable solution, pursued a different approach.

In highly creative thinkers who are constantly making novel associations, connections, and re-combinations, Fink found both lower levels of cortical activation and more alpha activity. He found that when a task required more creativity and when a subject's thinking got more original, the brain showed more alpha activity.

He took it a step further. In 2006, along with his colleagues Grabner, Benedek, and Neubauer, Fink conducted a study to determine if creativity training could change how people think. It was the first neuroscientific study of its kind. Half of the participants received training in divergent thinking, while the other half received none. After the training, the researchers actually saw and measured increases in the alpha activity of the trained group. Here, for the first time, was hard evidence that creativity training could alter brain function. Specifically, exercises such as word associations and writing challenges (activities that involve making and seeing connections) could increase alpha activity. They could actually make people more creative. How long before you could see the difference? Just two weeks!

British researchers recently found that alcohol, in the right amount, does tend to produce more creative thinking. Inspired by the latest data, the advertising agency Crispin Porter + Bogusky in Copenhagen created a new creativity beer. The label on the back of the bottle (inset) shows just how much you need to drink to get the desired effect.

How "normal" people think

Concept: Dorte Nielsen.

How highly creative people think

Concept: Dorte Nielsen.

The librarian and the conductor

From the studies on cognitive neuroscience, we know that thinking in "normal" people is more constrained, while thinking in the brains of highly creative people is more freewheeling. That's because the prefrontal cortex in highly creative thinkers is allowed to orchestrate the combination and recombination of elements found in the rest of the brain. A simple analogy illustrates what happens in our brains during creative thinking.

The librarian in the conventional thinker

Think of your brain as a huge library that serves as a resource for creative thought. At the help desk of the normal mind, you will find a librarian. Ask her for help researching the subject of cats, and she will politely point you toward to the encyclopedia that starts with "C." No detours or alternative suggestions are offered.

The conductor in the creative thinker

In the creative mind, roaming behind the help desk you will find, not a librarian, but a conductor, who orchestrates thought processes using the whole library, drawing on every conceivable resource, making remote combinations and far-fetched connections. Everything is at play at the same time. As a result, the thinking is unexpected, and more original ideas and unusual options spring to mind.

Train your inner librarian

The exciting news from the neuroscientists is that your librarian can be trained to act more like a conductor to explore the far-flung resources of your mental library. All it takes is some simple creativity training.
So the next time someone asks you to think outside the box, you can call on your prefrontal conductor to fetch the information you've stored up on trumpets, Mexican food, volcanic activity, how to knit socks for toddlers, and 18th century watercolors, and help you make connections to any given subject. For though we are all born with a particular brain, we know now that we all have the capacity to take our creative thinking to the next level through training.

Train your inner librarian

Concept: Dorte Nielsen.

Birdhouse by Andreas Green Lorentzen.

A quick course in creative thinking

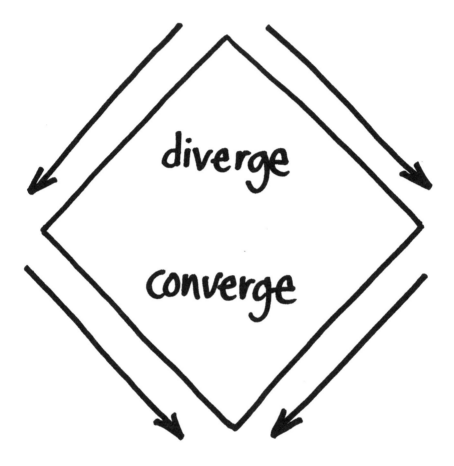

The creative heartbeat

When it comes to creative thinking, even the simple act of separating divergent and convergent thinking will help you come up with more and better ideas. The recent "Bus Study" from the International Center for Studies in Creativity shows that even people who were not trained in creative thinking produced significantly better solutions when asked to diverge first and converge later.

The heartbeat of creativity

Whether you consider yourself "creative" or not, creative thinking is a natural capacity of all human beings. There are predictable dynamics and knowable stages. Better still, there is a common language, and there are guidelines that can help us think and collaborate more effectively.

Like heartbeats and breathing, creative thinking has a natural and unconscious rhythm of its own. It expands and contracts: we instinctively open up the possibilities before we narrow our choices.

Psychologist J.P. Guilford called this phenomenon "divergent" and "convergent" thinking. He suggested that, to enhance our creative output, we should consciously separate the two.

Divergent thinking opens possibilities

Divergent thinking is all about expanding—generating lots of options, combining ideas, stretching for wild and unusual possibilities, all the while deferring judgment. It thrives in a state of dreamy, playful, defocused attention.

Divergent thinking is standing in front of an open refrigerator and considering all the things and endless combinations of things you could possibly eat for lunch.

Convergent thinking narrows the options

Convergent thinking is all about contracting, tossing out the off-target ideas, and focusing on the few on-target options that will really help you reach your objective. The trick to converging is to be deliberate about your choices and be sure you don't throw out all the novel options in your effort to be reasonable.

Convergent thinking is when you grab the ham and cheese, add the unexpected mango salad, and close the fridge.

In terms of creative connections, divergent thinking is when you connect to possibilities. Convergent thinking is when you connect the most promising possibilities to your goal.

Divergent and convergent thinking are the heartbeat of the creative process. The Yin and Yang. The Fred and Ginger. To do the dance, they need to work together, yet remain respectfully apart. First diverge. Then converge. That's what allows the blood flow of new thinking. If you judge every idea as it comes along, you'll be stepping on the toes of every new connection you could make.

Creating a climate for connection making

As the "O" in the advertising agency BBDO, Alex Osborn prized the creative output of his company. He believed creativity could be understood and cultivated.

Osborn made a careful study of his creative team, and in 1940, he coined the term "brainstorming." It described the approach the BBDO creative team used to come up with a new slogan or ad campaign. They would gather and toss ideas about. They'd play with concepts and tease out silly far-fetched connections. The atmosphere was free of harsh judgment, and the best ideas didn't come early. They were often the result of much banter, extraction, exaggeration, and extrusion.

The ads that resulted often looked simple, almost effortless—as if someone had simply had an "Aha!" moment in the shower. In fact, they were the product of intentional, intense divergent thinking.

Whether you love brainstorming or hate it, it's worth remembering that the point of brainstorming—and divergent thinking in general—is to spend enough time in a "safe" space for idea generation, so that you can get past the obvious ideas, push beyond the silly ideas, and start to explore where truly original connections and ideas are.

You can achieve that—in groups or on your own—by following the guidelines for diverging. First, defer judgment. Resist the temptation to show how clever you are by shredding a new idea to bits. Give the idea a chance. Show it mercy. Let it live. Use it to build other ideas and make new associations. Seek novelty. And don't stop diverging the first time your pen droops. Keep at it. Strive for quantity. The more options you have, the more connections you can make.

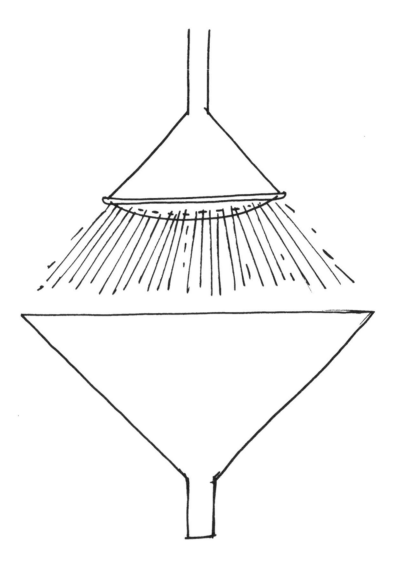

The Shower and the funnel

Think of divergent thinking like a shower of ideas. If the flow is too low, you'll only get a trickle of conventional ideas, just the usual suspects. If you turn up the flow, the spray goes wider and the ideas get more exploratory and more original. When it's time to converge, replace your shower with a funnel and drain away all but the very best.

Concept by Dorte Nielsen.

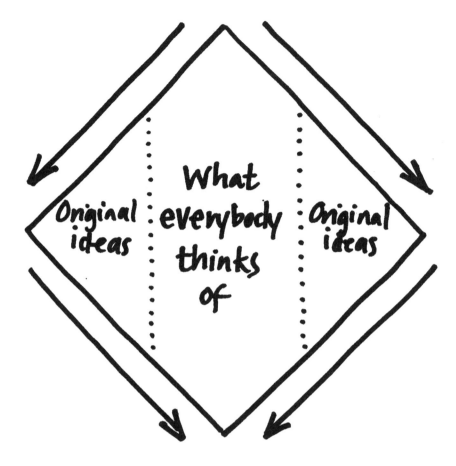

Original ideas

In this diagram of divergent and convergent thinking you can see that original ideas live on the edges, away from the ordinary ideas that sit in the middle. When you're trying to come up with a truly original idea, it often takes some hard rowing to pull yourself away from the ideas that everybody else is proposing. Learning to make connections is a skill that can help you pull away from the mainstream and point your thinking toward more distant associations where original ideas live.

Diagram (above) and guidelines (next page) from the book Creative Leadership by Puccio, Murdock, Mance.

The courage to converge

Most of us associate creativity with divergent thinking, but convergent thinking is every bit as important. Done badly, convergent thinking sounds like this: "Let's just go with what we did last year. It worked fine."

The evolution of our species has left us with a compulsive need for safety and a natural aversion to try new things. So new ideas and connections, even good ones, don't have a chance unless you intentionally give them one. That's where convergent thinking comes in.

It takes creative courage to opt for the original, untried choice. Good convergent choices can change the world. That's why convergent thinking has its own guidelines to help people do it well. The first guideline is "be affirmative," which is to say, focus what you want (not what you don't want) and emphasize what you like (not what you don't like) about your choices. Next, be sure that you're choosing an option that not only delights you but also meets your criteria of success. Third, be deliberate about your choice. This is your chance to get it right. And finally, keep novelty alive.

A creative solution is both novel and valuable. If you kill the novelty, you kill the creativity, and any chance of innovation.

Separate but equal modes of thinking

We know that divergent and convergent thinking are both essential components of creativity. But they're odd bedfellows. Psychologists have found that some people are irresistibly drawn to divergent thinking, while others favor convergent thinking.

Trouble arises when people who prefer different modes of thinking try to battle it out. Picture a team of divergent ad copywriters zinging ideas endlessly, while the account managers stand with crossed arms and pursed lips waiting for them to pick a path forward. The first group could diverge all day. The second won't be happy until a convergent decision gets made.

On the next page, the guidelines for divergent and convergent thinking help groups align their thinking, improve their creative collaboration and avoid shooting down ideas prematurely. They also apply when you're working solo.

Guidelines for
Divergent thinking

Defer judgment
Strive for quantity
Make connections
Seek novelty

wild card: Allow for incubation.

Guidelines for
Convergent thinking

Be affirmative

Check objectives

Be deliberate

Keep novelty alive

converge

wild card: Allow for incubation.

Sparkling Idea by Sofie Engelbrecht Simonsen

Divergent thinking and leadership

Divergent thinking is fun and exploratory. It's full of dead ends, red herrings, and ideas that will never see the light of day. In case you think it's all mental fluff and frivolity, let us share one more research finding.

In 2002, researchers Vincent, Decker, and Mumford were curious to see if they could find a statistical correlation between creativity and leadership. They set out to find exactly how, or if, creativity and leadership connect. The team purposefully chose a group of leaders that fell outside of our cultural idea of who is "creative." In fact, they chose military leaders and analyzed their responses to military challenges. The findings came as a surprise to everybody.

Going in, the researchers assumed that leadership would correlate directly with experience and intelligence (of the IQ variety). What they found instead was that leaders are the people who come up with the best solutions. Simple enough. People vote with their feet. The best solutions will get the most followers.

Where do great solutions come from? Again, the researchers assumed the finger would point to experience and intelligence. But the strongest correlation was to great ideas: Great ideas produced great solutions.

Where do great ideas come from? Experience? Intelligence? This was the biggest surprise of all: according to the statistical analysis, great ideas come from divergent thinking, the ability to think fluently, flexibly and originally, the ability to explore untried, undervalued, untested, and unimagined options, the ability to do just the sort of thing we're talking about in this book.

The statistics showed that great leaders come from great solutions, great solutions come from great ideas, and great ideas come from divergent thinking. What ever happened to experience and intelligence? They still figure prominently in the play, but they work in direct support of divergent thinking, not in direct support of leadership.

Part 3

Enhance your innate creativity

Here's where you get to roll up your sleeves and train your ability to see and make connections. A few starter exercises will get you in the right frame of mind. Then it's time to tackle twenty-one exercises that will help you enhance your innate creativity.

Photograph by Dorte Nielsen

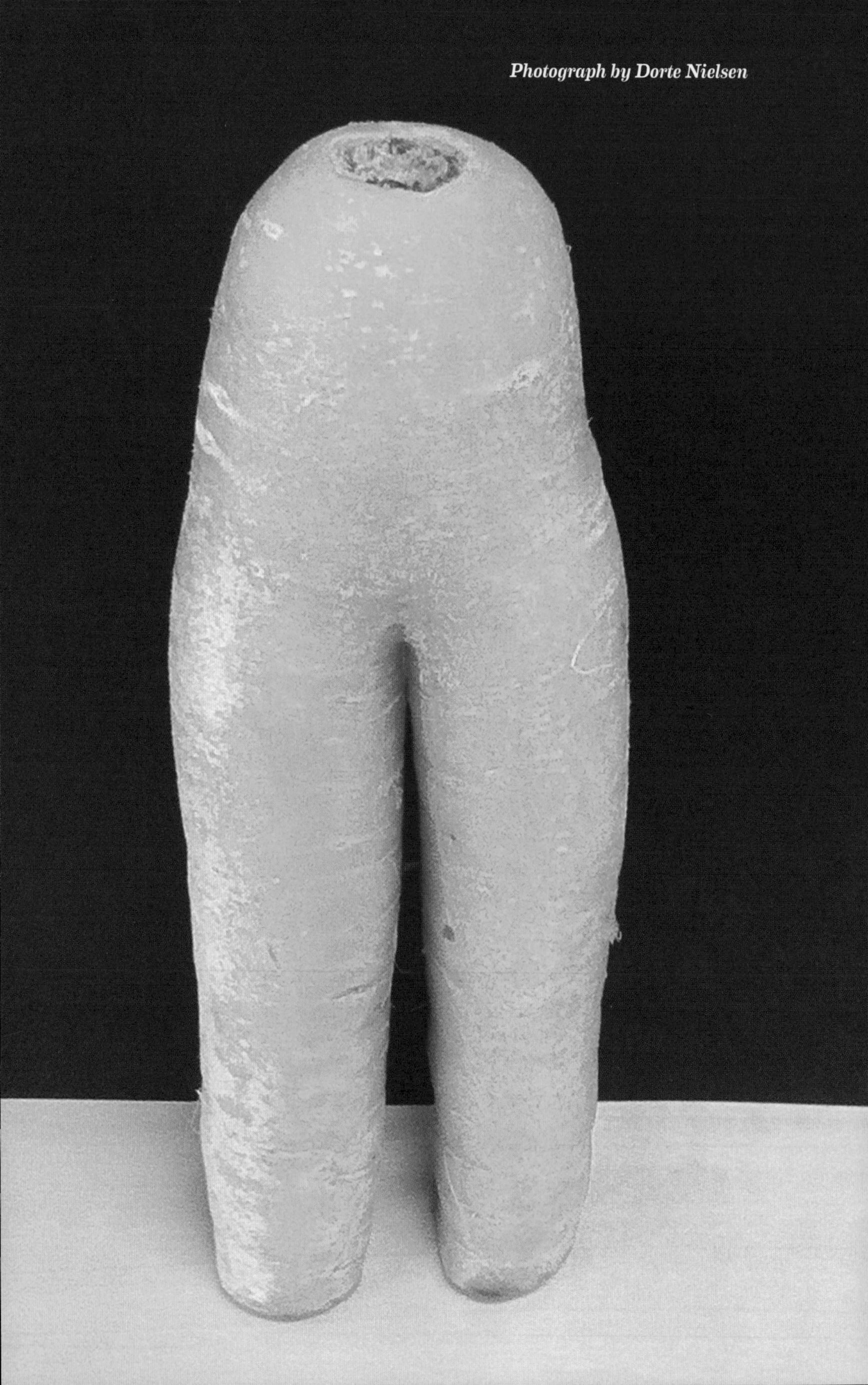

Train your ability to see connections

Can creativity be taught?

After teaching creativity for nearly twenty years, E. Paul Torrance got tired of people telling him "Creativity can't be taught." So he decided to tackle the question head on. He undertook a meta-analytic review of all the credible research studies he could find that asked the question: Can creativity be taught?

In 1972, after reviewing 142 studies of the effectiveness of creativity training (many of which relied on his Torrance Tests of Creative Thinking), he concluded, "It does indeed seem possible to teach creative thinking."

The aggregate results showed that creativity training improved performance on divergent thinking tests and produced reasonably large gains, especially in terms of originality.

Raising the level of creativity

In 1984, researchers Laura Hall Rose and Hsin-tai Lin ran another meta-analytic review, evaluating the effects of creativity training on divergent thinking scores. Some training programs, they found, were more effective than others, but overall they concluded:

"Creative thinking is at once a skill that can be developed through various teaching methodologies and an innate ability that some individuals have in greater abundance than others. This dual nature of creativity is not a contradiction of human development but an affirmation of the flexibility and malleability of individual potential. Through education and training the innate creative thinking ability of individuals can be stimulated and nourished."

So people are born with different levels of creativity. Training can raise that level, whatever its starting point. While creativity training does not guarantee creative output, it does appear to increase the odds.

Teaching creative connections

When you train your ability to see connections, you will actually increase your innate creative capacity. You will learn to think the way highly creative people think.

The skill of making connections can change your brain. Here's what happens in terms of fluency, flexibility, originality, and elaboration, the four basic creative characteristics that Torrance measures in his test.

Creative fluency

You will naturally increase your idea production by training your ability to combine thoughts and ideas. Research shows that the best way to have great ideas is to have a lot of ideas. This approach will help.

Creative flexibility

You will learn not to shy away from unusual connections that can help you shift gears, try new perspectives, consider other frames of reference, and embrace new strategies.

Creative originality

You will learn to find unexpected sources of inspiration, which tend to produce ideas that no one else has thought of.

Creative elaboration

Using your newfound skills of fluency, flexibility, and originality, you can use your new steady flow of ideas to help you embellish, refine and optimize your initial idea.

By training your brain to make connections consciously, you give your brain permission to make connections unconsciously. And you become a more creative thinker.

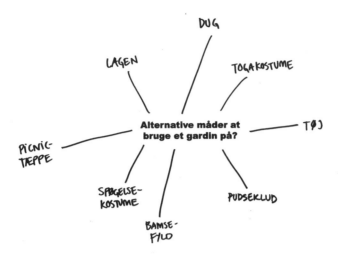

After a three-week course on creative connections, this particular Danish student produced nearly three times as many ideas for the same style of exercise as she did before she began the course (above and below).

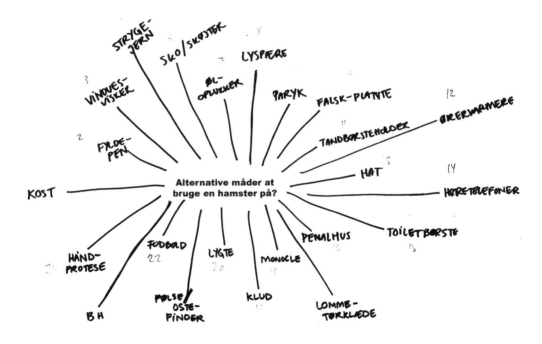

1001 ideas

The Creative Communications program at the Danish School of Media and Journalism is a three-year bachelor's program in communications and conceptual thinking. Halfway through the first year, students take a three-week intensive course called "1001 ideas." In essence, it's a three-week boot camp on the art of seeing and making connections. This is where their idea production takes off.

Before and after

It starts with a pretest, in which students have to list alternative uses for a familiar household item. At the end of the three weeks, for most students, idea production doubles. For some it triples. The students themselves feel the change. In a self-assessment they rate the shift in their capacity for thinking creatively. Without exception, every score goes up. Even the most gifted idea generators find the exercises useful. They say the repeated exposure to connection making helps them see their own internal creative mechanism at work. Going forward, they know they can call on their creativity when they need it, because connection making can help them find inspiration anytime, anywhere.

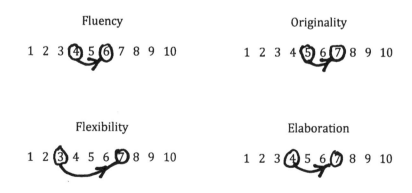

Fluency

1 2 3 ④ 5 ⑥ 7 8 9 10

Originality

1 2 3 4 ⑤ 6 ⑦ 8 9 10

Flexibility

1 2 ③ 4 5 6 ⑦ 8 9 10

Elaboration

1 2 3 ④ 5 6 ⑦ 8 9 10

Students reported an increase in creative capacity in their self assessment.

Before you begin

Enough of being an armchair observer of creative connections. Now it's time for you to start making connections of your own. Remember, you're building a skill and skill building takes time. Be patient and persistent. As you complete the exercises in this book, you will start to notice more connections around you. You will find inspiration in connections. And with work, and a little luck, your connections will lead you to new ideas, clever inventions, and personal breakthroughs.

A connections notebook

Before you begin, we encourage you to get your own "connections notebook." Your notebook is a place to collect your thoughts, concepts, observations, and new connections. It's a place to paste in pictures of things that inspire you. It's a place to write your reflections and "Aha!" moments. It's a place to record signs of progress. Plus, it will be a handy place to write down your answers to the challenges and exercises in the next part of this book. We recommend using a notebook with unlined pages. Look for something large enough to sketch and write in, but small enough to carry around.

Three challenges to launch your journey

While the twenty-one exercises in boot camp will give you quick daily hits of connection making, there are three special challenges we'll ask you to do before those begin.

> Challenge 1: The walk
> Challenge 2: A walk with a purpose
> Challenge 3: Source of inspiration

These challenges will take a little longer than the daily boot camp exercises. They are designed to help you sink a little deeper into the connection-making mindset. Think of them as indoctrination rituals to get your head in the right frame of mind.

Pacman by Mikkel Moller

How to start seeing connections

Seeing connections is a mindset, a way of looking at the world. It's an ability you can train. Once you start focusing on making connections, they will come to you from all kinds of places, expected and unexpected.

When you get the hang of it, you will easily see a connection between a mitten and a mailbox, a ceiling fan and a karate chop. And those connections, inspired by all kinds of new and interesting sources, will help you gain insights and solve problems.

You can't make a creative connection by simply looking. Creative connections happen only when you truly see. Looking is passive. It's the brain in neutral gear. Seeing is active. It happens when all the wheels are spinning in your brain. Remember how Pablo Picasso saw a bull in a bike? And how photographer Elliott Erwitt saw some wonderful female attributes in two gourds?

Creative people see what everyone else is looking at, and they create something completely different, because they connect the dots differently.

Connections mark the moment of creative conception. They happen when you suddenly connect knowledge, observation, and experience in your brain in a new way. The more random knowledge you collect, the more original the connections you can make. That's why so many creative thinkers fill their brains with reading, travel, adventure, and input from odd places and unexpected sources. It increases their odds of making novel connections.

As a student, Mikkel Møller took the train to school. Every day he stood behind the dotted line that marked where the train would pull up. Most people took no notice, but Mikkel saw a connection. One day he added a Pacman to the end of the dotted line. That day, everyone rode the train with a smile, because of the new way Mikkel had connected the dots.

Winter Observation by Dorte Nielsen

Observation

The trick is to follow the advice of National Geographic photographer Dewitt Jones: "Look at the ordinary and see the extraordinary."

You can train your ability to look beyond the ordinary. Of course, you'll have to create some personal time to do it. Start by becoming a better observer.

Good observers take in details. Where you might normally just brush past, slow down a bit to notice the world around you.

Take time to smell the roses. Then look carefully at their petal structure, at their thorns, and the fringes of their leaves. Find something about the rose that surprises you. Something you hadn't noticed before. Could that thorn be a fang? A fingernail cleaner? A foot grip for walking on ice?

That's how highly creative people work. They make connections.

Look at the world with a new set of eyes. Go for walks. Observe. The more you do it, the easier it gets. And suddenly tree stumps begin to look like Darth Vader.

Looking at the world in this way is fundamental to becoming better at seeing connections. Why not make it a daily or weekly habit? Take some personal time and go for observational walks on your own.

Challenge 1
The walk

Thinkers from Einstein to Emerson were great believers in taking a walk. The American writer Gretel Ehrlich noted, "Walking is also an ambulation of mind." The walk we want you to take is no ordinary walk. This walk is a chance to look at the world and see it differently.

Tips for the walk
- Bring a notebook and a camera along.
- Look at things and think of what they might be or could be.
- Photograph objects and scenes that spur your imagination.
- Imagine new combinations and connections.
- Jot down at least ten ideas (e.g. how to turn a gutter pipe into an airport hangar or a lawn mower into a jewelry box, etc.).

Recommendation
Do this on your own. Give yourself a block of time (anywhere from sixty to ninety minutes). Focus on seeing new things when you look at ordinary things. Focus on having ideas. Don't try to do your grocery shopping at the same time or walk the dog or have a phone conversation. This time is for you and your thinking.

Bonus activity
Choose a photograph from your walk and create a "before" and "after" picture series to show the image you saw and the vision you created.

On the opposite page, you can see the connection that Louise Arve made on her walk between some old water pipes and the hooves of a horse.

Horse by Louise Arve

Helping Hands
by Simone Wärme

Observation as an inspiration

With practice, your observations of the world around you will become an ongoing source of inspiration. But there are other places to look for inspiration. One of the most fruitful places is problems.

Life's little problems

Start to see life's little everyday problems as an invitation to invent, rather than as a cause to complain. Problems are where the gold is. Notice when the soap gets in your eyes, when the trash bag splits, or when you hit your finger with a hammer. Problems are a perfect playground for creative connections.

John Montagu, the fourth Earl of Sandwich, loved to play cards. The problem was, he couldn't eat while playing without the risk of getting greasy meat stains on the cards. Then he made a clever connection. Bread would be the perfect blotter. He asked his servant to bring his meat between two slices of bread. Soon other card players began to request the same as Sandwich. You can thank the Earl the next time you eat one.

Creativity guru Sid Parnes recognized that part of our failure to recognize problems as creative opportunities stems from the way we talk about them. We tend to grumble about problems as fixed, chronic complaints. "My dog has fleas." "My kids spend too much time on screens." Parnes believed that flipping the language could unblock the problem. Specifically, reframing problems as open-ended questions could invite the brain to make new connections. His magic phrase was "How might I..." How might I get rid of my dog's fleas? How might I encourage my kids to spend less time on screens? Suddenly the mind is open, looking for connections.

The next time you bike home from the grocery store and think: "How might I get an extra pair of hands?" consider inventing one, as Simone Wärme did.

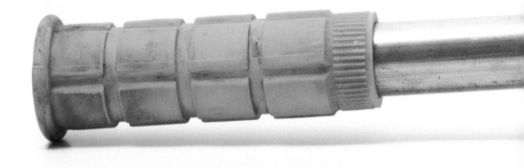

Solving for life's little problems, Sebastian Risom Drejer designed a new tool: a nail holder that keeps you from hitting your finger with a hammer.

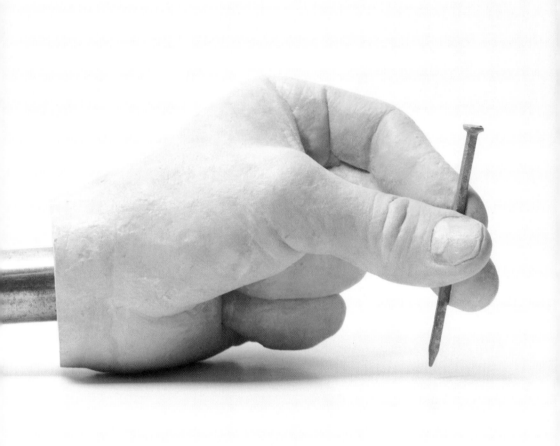

A great observation became a clever solution when Mikkel Moller turned a pencil shaving into a Christmas card for the Creative Communication department.

Challenge 2
A walk with a purpose

Once you've trained your mind to see connections for the fun of it, you're ready to go a step further and put your new skill to work. Start using your ability to see connections as a way to solve problems and tackle challenges.

Observation as an inspiration

On your next walk, bring a challenge along. The creative connections you make may provide you with insights and ideas, new perspectives and possible solutions that you hadn't thought of before.

Simply switch on your creative thinking cap, focus on an everyday object and ask, "What ideas does this object give me to help me address my challenge?"

Let what you observe prompt your brain to consider the object's characteristics. Say you spot a fire hydrant: It's short, sturdy, and tough. It's ready in an emergency. You can't park in front of it. Dogs pee on it. Any of those characteristics could spark a connection that can help you address the challenge at hand.

This method of making random connections is a classic creativity tool, variously known as Forced Connections or Random Input. It's also a trick well known by highly creative people. In an interview for the book *Inspired*, fashion designer Paul Smith said, "Inspiration comes from observation. I get inspiration from seeing things that are out of context. It could be a Ferrari parked outside a fourteenth-century monastery. The fact that they clash with each other could be the inspiration for combining a denim shirt with a cashmere suit, or putting a modern chair in a traditional environment."

"I try to look for inspiration where you wouldn't necessarily expect to find it. If I have a brief for a film, I don't go and look at other films, but at public transport or art."

Rob Wagemans, Architect

Inspiration

Highly creative people have to keep their creative juices flowing. Early on in their careers, they naturally look to others in their field. Painters go to gallery openings. Writers read novels. Architects travel the world looking at beautiful buildings. As a learner, it's logical to be inspired by the best in your field. You need to understand the canon or cultural meme. But be careful. If the achievements in your field are your only sources of inspiration, you'll be drawing inspiration from the same connection-making pool as everyone else.

If your work is going to be original, you need to understand the meme, and then you need to break it.

Creative professionals know this. In order to trigger ideas that are really original, they go outside their field to find inspiration. Connecting with people, objects, experiences, or cultures outside the normal sweep of their field is what gives them inspired creativity.

"I try to look for inspiration were you wouldn't necessarily expect to find it," architect Rob Wagemans confided in an interview in the book, *Inspired*. "If I have a brief for a film, I don't go and look at other films, but at public transport or art."

Creative professionals who can deliberately tap their ability to see connections have confidence they can find inspiration in everything. Connection making sustains their creative freshness. Creative professionals who don't know this often live in secret anxiety, feeling they have to keep pulling creative ideas out of their own heads. They live in fear of creative blocks and burnout.

Knowing that your sources of inspiration are infinite means that your job as a creative person is to build your connection-making machinery. Once you are able to make connections, all you are missing is the next trigger. The world becomes your oyster of creative inspiration, and there is no end to what you can do.

An environmentally friendly rainwater collector inspired August Laustsen to create his own personal water collection device.

Challenge 3
The source of inspiration

Inspiration comes from observations, problems, and an infinite number of other sources. Different people draw inspiration from different things.

What inspires you? By paying attention to what happens when a creative idea comes to you, you are more likely to do it again. Where does your inspiration come from? Art? Music? Nature? Machine parts? Fabrics? Architecture? Fresh ingredients? Nearly anything can inspire a creative connection. Over the years, we've found it's worth asking people to dwell on this. It helps them tap into and return to their own unique sources of inspiration.

1. Think of something you created. Now think of what inspired you to create it.

2. Take a photograph or draw a sketch of both your creation and your inspiration.

3. Attach the images side by side to a sheet of paper (or a page in your connection notebook). Put your inspiration on the left and your creation on the right.

4. Under the images, write a brief reflection on what happened when you created what you did. Did you look at one thing and suddenly see something else? Describe what happened for you.

"You can find inspiration in everything."

Paul Smith, fashion designer

Star Wars inspired Kasper Dohlmann to transform the glaring florescent light in his friend's kitchen into a light saber. He painted Yoda's figure on the wall behind it to complete the effect.

The elegant movements of a ballet dancer inspired Line Schou to create a new design. First she traced the movements of the dancer. Then she designed the type.

Boot Camp

Welcome to boot camp

Welcome to creative connection boot camp! The twenty-one exercises that follow will enhance your ability to see connections. Simply reading these exercises is about as useful as sitting on a couch and watching a workout video. You might like it, but it won't do much for you.

As you flick through the exercises (you are allowed to flick through), you'll see they are numbered one to twenty-one. An icon marks the beginning of each exercise. A time estimate gives you a sense of how long it will take.

Some exercises look quite similar to each other. They are. Like any form of exercise, you have to do them over and over to get the maximum benefit. That said, you'll find an array of visual, verbal, and conceptual exercises to keep things fresh.

Verbal exercises

Some of the exercises focus on seeing verbal connections through stories and word games. If writing is not your strong suit, don't worry. It's the connections, not the writing, that matter.

Visual exercises

Likewise, you don't have to draw well to complete the visual exercises. Stick figures are just fine. But try to draw, it calls on a different type of thinking and prompts new thoughts and connections.

Conceptual exercises

These exercises focus on ideas, thoughts, and conceptual thinking.

The boot camp is designed as a three-week course with twenty-one exercises. One for everyday.

The exercises generally take between ten to fifteen minutes. Allow time and be patient with yourself. You're asking your brain to think a whole new way. The exercises will kick start your connection making. You'll start seeing connections all over.

If you are enjoying working on an exercise, don't worry too much about the suggested time frame; just take as long as you like.

If you didn't create one earlier, now is the time to start your own "Connections Workbook" to record and collect your responses in one spot. Any style of notebook will work.

The aim of the exercises is not to create the best and most original ideas for each exercise, but to train your brain to see and make more connections. After training, and a bit of practice, the great and original ideas will come more easily.

Alternative approaches

While we have suggested doing one exercise a day for three weeks, you can do the boot camp any way that suits you. You can do the exercises in order or at random. Do one a week or one a day. Wake up fifteen minutes earlier and do an exercise every Monday through Friday. Or do five in a row every Saturday and Sunday. Whatever works for you. If you do the exercises, that's where the value is.

Remember what the neuroscientists found? Divergent exercises like these can change people's brain activity in only two weeks. We've given you twenty-one days of exercises. That's long enough not only to change your thinking, but to change your thinking habits. Our goal is to help you build more fluency, flexibility, originality, and elaboration into your daily thoughts. These exercises really will change your mind.

Exercise 1
Alternative uses

10-15 minutes

Thinking of alternative uses for an object is a way to train your mind to make new connections. It limbers up your thinking by asking you to stretch beyond the obvious uses and imagine the object outside of its usual context.

Challenge yourself to seek some really wacky uses. Remember humor is a great muse for creativity.

For each object, take exactly three minutes. Write down as many alternative uses as you can for a

Pot lid

Bicycle tire

Empty ketchup bottle

Candle

Some researchers consider people's ability to think of alternative uses as a way to measure their creative ability. The more you train your capacity to think of alternative uses, the better you get. Save this exercise so you can check your progress at the end of boot camp.

Here's an alternative use for a coffin by Sune Overby Sørensen and an alternative and very practical use for a dog bone by Camilla Berlick.

"I invented nothing new. I simply combined the inventions of others into a car."

Henry Ford

Exercise 2
The bike

10-15 minutes

When Picasso looked at a bike, he saw a bull. Most of the time, when we look at a bike, we see a bike.

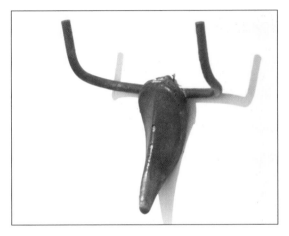

The aim of this exercise is to look at a bike and not think "bike" but think of as many other things as possible.

1. Alternative uses: On the next page you'll see all kinds of bike parts. Look them over. Take your time. Then, for each part, write down as many ideas as you can imagine for alternative uses, inventions, or artistic creations.

2. New combinations: Now picture the different parts of the bike in different combinations and create even more new things.

Remember, you are not trying to solve a problem. You are trying to look at things differently in order to create something new.

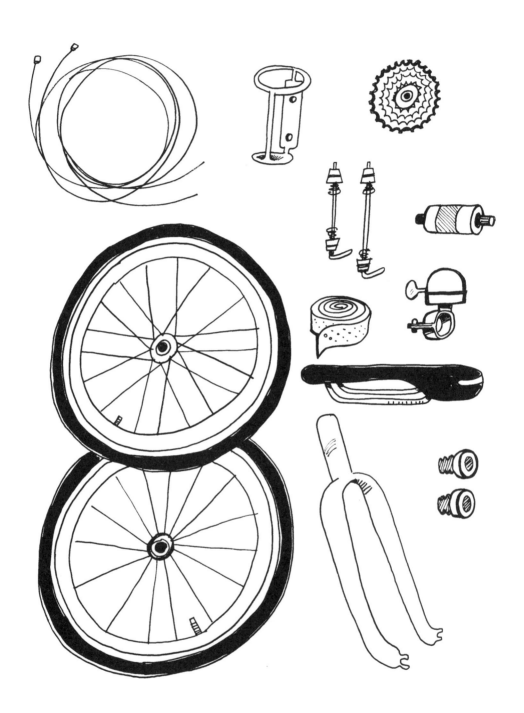

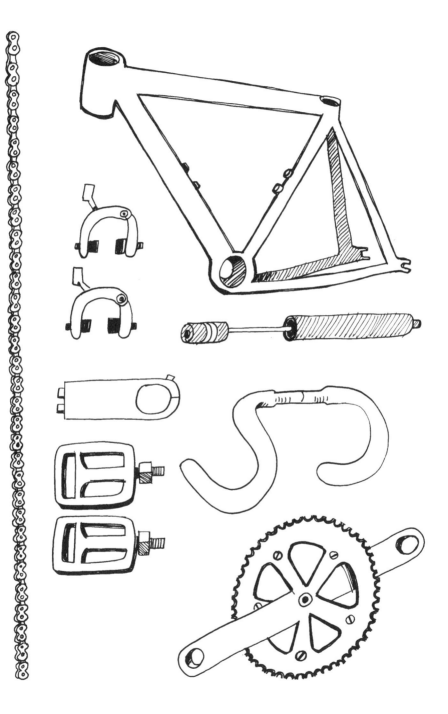

Here is an example of how this exercise can be done.

Exercise 3
Visual connections 1

10-15 minutes

Think of the grid below as a visual multiplication table. Your job is to look at each blank square and figure out how the two visuals connect. Draw a picture to illustrate your idea. Don't worry about the quality of your drawing. Just think and draw!

Work sheet to be photocopied. Adjust size to fit paper. Nielsen & Thurber.

Exercise 4
Visual connections 2

10-15 minutes

Try this exercise again. (You get better at it.) This time, the prompts are words. Combine the two words and draw your idea in the empty box.

?	Book	Shoe
Dog		
Worm		
Key		

What do you get if you cross a cow with a trampoline?

Exercise 5
Jokes

10-15 minutes

Why jokes? We do these exercises because this particular genre of jokes is built on connections.

- What do you get if you cross A with B?
- What's the difference between A and B?
- What do A and B have in common?

Laughter ensues because the connection invariably goes wrong. It's ironic, absurd, or totally unexpected.

At first, these jokes can be really hard to solve, but as you pay attention to the way the connections work, your brain will begin to get the hang of it. The trick is to look for unique characteristics of each item and start crisscrossing to find amusing unexpected connections.

For example, "What do you get when you cross a shark with a parrot?" One distinguishing attribute of a shark is they bite off limbs. One distinguishing trait of a parrot is they talk. Connect those two attributes and you get the answer: A bird that will talk your ear off. The common phrase "talk your ear off" has absurdly laughable implications when you remember there's a shark involved.

These exercises are a great springboard to making your own connections. First, go through them and try to guess the answer to each joke. Even if you miss it, take a minute to identify the characteristics that combined to make the joke work. Then spend some time trying to write a few jokes of your own. Crack the code and you'll be up to your eyeballs in connections.

What do you get when you cross?

1. What do you get when you cross a cow with a trampoline?

2. What do you get when you cross a burger with a computer?

3. What do you get when you cross a parrot with a centipede?

4. What do you get when you cross the devil with roller skates?

5. What do you get when you cross a genius with a chicken?

6. What do you get when you cross a bull and a baker?

7. What do you get when you cross Fido with a mosquito bite?

8. What do you get when you cross a lawyer with a garden mole?

9. What do you get when you cross a wizard with the Sahara?

10. What do you get when you cross 5th Avenue with a poodle?

Now try writing a few jokes of your own.

What do you get when you cross a _____ with _____?

Woodpecker by Lea Brisell.
Tandem Slippers by Camilla Søholt Larsen.

Suggestions

There's never just one right answer. But here's some suggestions to what an answer could be. Maybe you have a better suggestion or a different suggestion?

1. A milkshake

2. A big Mac

3. A walkie-talkie

4. Hell on wheels

5. A fowl mind

6. A cow pie

7. A son of an itch

8. Blind justice

9. A dry spell

10. You get to the other side of 5th Avenue*

* Notice that the answer to the last question is funny only because it breaks the pattern unexpectedly. Instead of combining the traits of the two items, the joke surprises you with a literal answer.

Exercise 6
Making headlines

10-15 minutes

Here's another storytelling exercise. Imagine a news story that could somehow include and connect all five images below. Look them over carefully. Think about how the images could be connected in a newspaper article.

Take ten to twelve minutes to write a newspaper headline and caption that incorporates all five images.

Exercise 7
The RAT

10-15 minutes

The Remote Associates Test (RAT) was developed by Martha and Sarnoff Mednick in 1962. It measures a fundamental creative ability: making verbal connections.

The RAT test is based on words. The task is to look at three given words and find or think of a fourth word that connects to each of the three.

For example, you could be given the three words:

Birthday   Surprise   Line

It's then your task to find a fourth word that connects to each of them.

In this case the answer is "party" because you can add the word party to all three of the other words, as in birthday party, surprise party, and party line. Notice that the fourth word can either go in front of or behind each of the given words.

For a quick test of your verbal flexibility, try to find a fourth word that connects the three words in each of the rows on the next page.

Disclaimer

This test is much harder than it looks. Some of the associations may not come to you at all. Don't despair, and don't let it knock the confidence out of you. Although this was originally written to be a creativity test, some of the most artistic, visual, and conceptual thinkers we know fail miserably at it.

Try the RAT

1. rocking	wheel	high	_Chair_
2. cottage	Swiss	cake	
3. cream	skate	water	
4. show	life	row	
5. night	wrist	stop	
6. duck	fold	dollar	
7. ranger	preserve	tropical	
8. aid	rubber	wagon	
9. flake	mobile	cone	
10. cracker	fly	fighter	
11. safety	cushion	point	
12. cane	daddy	plum	
13. dream	break	light	
14. fish	mine	rush	
15. political	surprise	line	
16. measure	worm	video	

The RAT: Suggested answers

1. rocking wheel high *chair*

2. cottage Swiss cake *cheese*

3. cream skate water *ice*

4. show life row *boat*

5. night wrist stop *watch*

6. duck fold dollar *bill*

7. ranger preserve tropical *forest*

8. aid rubber wagon *band*

9. flake mobile cone *snow*

10. cracker fly fighter *fire*

11. safety cushion point *pin*

12. cane daddy plum *sugar*

13. dream break light *day*

14. fish mine rush *gold*

15. political surprise line *party*

16. measure worm video *tape*

Exercise 8
Random visuals

10-15 minutes

Time for more practice in making visual connections! Look at the images below and fill in the empty boxes with drawings that illustrate your idea of how the two corresponding items might connect.

Exercise 9
Shoes +

10-15 minutes

Once again, your job is to challenge your brain to connect two things that don't naturally go together.

Start with a shoe. Combine it with the following items to create something new. This exercise is about fluency, so your ideas don't have to be practical or original. Focus instead on creating a lot of different ideas. Try to come up with at least five combinations of a shoe and each of the following items:

Lamp

Pepper grinder

Flower pot

Banana

Necktie

Umbrella

Wine bottle

Lego Shoes by Jesper Wendelbo Lindeløv.
All Terrain Shoes by René Schultz.

Exercise 10
The movie blurb

10-15 minutes

In this exercise, imagine you are writing a screenplay and you want to entice people to watch the movie. Look at the ten words below. Choose five. Discover a connection between them, and write a gripping movie blurb.

Here's an example of a movie blurb from *The Return of the Street Fighter* that you can use for inspiration: "Sonny Chiba returns as a mercenary. This time he's out to bust up a phony charity. But who can he trust? It seems everyone is in on the plot, even his trusty sidekick, Kitty. Soon Terry finds himself up against many unexpected enemies, such as his old karate teacher."

Exercise 11
Story window

10-15 minutes

Here are nine images. You will be asked to write a story using five. Think about how the various images could be connected. What is a story that combines the images? Notice how the story changes depending on which images you choose.

Once you decide on your five images, find a connection between the pictures that inspires you, and write the story.

Here is an example of how this exercise can be done.

Exercise 12
Visual elaboration 1

10-15 minutes

This exercise looks like visual connections, but instead of connecting multiple different items, you must connect the same two items in multiple ways. It helps develop the creative skill of elaboration. Fill in each box with a unique illustration.

shoe		
		sun

Work sheet to be photocopied. Adjust size to fit paper. Nielsen & Thurber.

Exercise 13
Visual elaboration 2

10-15 minutes

Let's try this again. Remember, you're flexing your muscles for originality and elaboration, which are both critical to creative thinking. Look at the two words in the boxes and draw how those items might be connected or combined.

frame		
		snake

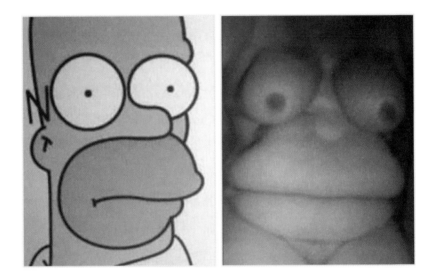

What do Homer Simpson and your wife have in common?
This extraordinary observation of a connection went viral when it was posted
on the Internet.

Exercise 14
In common

10-15 minutes

1. What do ski resorts and pantyhose have in common?

2. What do fluorescent tubes and librarians have in common?

3. What do Bermuda shorts and sermons have in common?

4. What do campsites and movies have in common?

5. What do babies and basketball players have in common?

6. What do freckles and bad neighborhoods have in common?

7. What do balloons and virgins have in common?

8. What do duct tape and gravity have in common?

9. What do Dracula and a lollipop have in common?

10. What do Alexander the Great, John the Baptist, and Winnie the Pooh all have in common?

Now try writing a few jokes of your own.

What do _____ and _____ have in common?

Suggestions

1. Runs

2. They glare

3. They are both long

4. Trailers

5. They both dribble

6. They're spotty

7. One prick and its gone

8. They hold the universe together

9. They're both suckers

10. The same middle name

Exercise 15
Reverse thinking

10-15 minutes

Here's an alternative uses exercise with a twist. Choose an item. As a warm up, do three minutes of alternative uses for your item, answering the question, What else could my item do?

Now you're ready. This time, write a list of all the things that your item doesn't do. For example:

> It doesn't fly me to the moon.
> It doesn't smell like freshly baked bread.
> It doesn't help with my cleaning.

Write a list of at least ten things your item doesn't do.

Once you get a complete list of failures, reverse it. Instead of writing what your item doesn't do, start the sentence "How might my item..." For instance:

> How might my item take me to the moon?
> How might my item smell like freshly baked bread?
> How might my item help with cleaning?

People often find it much easier to come up with things their item doesn't do, perhaps because that requires critical thinking, and we're all trained to do that. The trick is to leverage your critical thinking, then flip it to creative thinking.

Notice that when you are intentionally picking the things your item is least suited for, when you flip the failure into a question, the answers you get are often more crazy, far-fetched, and original.

Alternative uses of a chicken by Andrew Smart.

Exercise 16
Alternative uses 2

10-15 minutes

Here you see many alternative uses for a chicken.

1. From your current surroundings, choose three items for
    which you can create alternative uses.

2. Start with one of the items. Think of as many things as
    you possibly can. Take your time.

3. If you start to run dry, start to combine your item with
    other things (using random connections).

To spark more ideas, start to ask questions such as:

*   What problems might my chosen item solve?
*   What would be the cruelest thing to use my item for?
*   How could I make my item into a pleasant surprise?

Create more questions of your own to spark more ideas.

Whenever you run a bit dry for ideas for alternative uses, switch to the
next of the three items. Once you have done all three. Start with the
first of again. And why not, mix the first one with the second one?

When thoughts start to slow down again, look once more at all the
alternative uses of a chicken. See if that sparks new thoughts for your
item.

CANDLE STICK

Exercise 17
Visual puns

10-15 minutes

In advertising, puns are generally frowned upon. They tend to be silly or banal. Just perfect for what we're after, because puns are born of connections. Specifically, they exploit the multiple possible meanings of words, sounds or thoughts. What makes them funny is that they choose the unconventional meaning. "I used to be a banker, but I lost interest." "Camping is intense." As such, puns exercise exactly the same muscle you're working on to make connections.

In this exercise, rather than create the more common *verbal* pun, your job is to draw a literal and unexpected *visual* interpretation of the following words:

Grandfather clock

Hand luggage

Lighthouse

Basketball

Spring mattress

Butterfly

Hammerhead

Visual puns: Football Boot by René Schultz. Running Shoes by Casper Christensen. Candle Stick by Mads Haugsted Rasmussen.

Exercise 18
MisSPell, your new muse

10-15 minutes

Computers can be a source of creative inspiration, if you know how to use them. In this exercise, we rely on the inspiration of spell check to provide a random muse to interrupt and redirect the story. On a computer with spell check, start to write a story beginning with:

"It was a dark and stormy night ..."

However, make sure you misspell some of the words. So your opening sentence could read:

"It was a yark and sormy niyht ..."

When you ask spell check for suggestions, you'll find that yark could be york, yak, yard, yarn, or yank. Sormy could be stormy, sorry or wormy. Niyht could be night or knight. Any of those alternate choices can transform your story and take it down a whole new path. Your new sentence could now read:

"It was a dark and sorry knight ..."

Let's try this out. On a computer, start writing: "It was a dark and stormy night ..." Once you've written a paragraph or two, go back and misspell a few choice words. Look them up on spell check. Exchange the misspelled words with ones that spell check recommends. Exchange at least five words. Then read you text again, and let the new version of your story inspire you to write on. Whenever you feel stuck, you use spell check as your random input machine to bring new life into your storyline. Remember the aim of the exercise is to train your ability to make connections and be flexible in your thinking, not to write an award-winning novel. But who knows, once spell check has destroyed your creative Madonna, maybe you will.

It was a yark and sormy niyht ...

Exercise 19
In the kitchen

10-15 minutes

This exercise is a variation on alternative uses. It trains your ability to see connections by asking you to bring a strange item into a familiar context, your kitchen.

Start by thinking of three items you would like to work with (for example, a lawn mower, a bagpipe and a hamster.) Take your workbook, and go into your kitchen. Sit down. Find inspiration in all the magical things we use to mix and chop and flavor food in the kitchen. Choose one of your three items, and start to create alternative uses for it, inspired by what you find.

Let's say you have chosen to work on a hamster. Then it might help you to ask questions such as:

How might I use a hamster to stir the sauce in the pan?
How might I use a hamster as a salt dispenser?
How might I use a hamster to do the dishes?
How might I use a hamster as a doorstopper?
How might I use a hamster to crush garlic?
How might I use a hamster to prevent red wine stains?

As a warm up, substitute one of your items for the word hamster and answer the questions above. Draw or make a list of your ideas. Now look around your kitchen and find alternative uses for your other two items.

Corkscrew mouse by Line Johnsen. Cheesecake by Eva Stehr Ebbensgaard.

Exercise 20
Roll and write

10-15 minutes

The four categories "Who, When, Where, and What" are the key ingredients of your story. Under each category, there are six alternatives. Roll a die to determine which item under each category goes into your story. Try not to cheat. Then write the story.

Who?

1. A bus conductor and a stranger

2. A pole dancer and her mother

3. A college professor and a kindergartener

4. An inventor and a janitor

5. A star and a fan

6. A bank teller and a fortune teller

Where?

1. In the Eiffel tower in Paris

2. At a shopping mall

3. On Wall Street

4. At the opera

5. A casino

6. On safari

What?

1. A misunderstanding

2. Something important went down the drain

3. An explosion

4. A bad hair day

5. There's a blizzard

6. A homicide

When?

1. In the middle of the night

2. The 18th century

3. 2050

4. At the crack of dawn

5. During a nap

6. When the mail comes

Two new ways to use a chicken by Andrew Smart.

Exercise 21
Alternative uses finale

10-15 minutes

Now you've come to the final exercise, and you'll find it looks familiar. That's intentional. This is your chance to see how far you've come and to see how much fluency, flexibility, and originality you've gained. (We're sure it's quite a lot, not to put any pressure on you.)

So this time, in this alternative uses exercise, take three minutes for each item and push yourself to think of as many alternative used for it as possible.

Water bottle

Mouse

Brick

Rolling pin

When you're done, pull out the paper you saved from Exercise 1 and take a look.

Part Four

Putting connections to work

Here are a few classic connection-making tools that will help you put your newfound skills to work. They will come in handy when the pressure is on to make creative connections in a real-world context.

Happy Hour by
Marie Christine Frederiksen

Time to
celebrate

*"It's not where you
take things from,
it's where you take
them to."*

Jean-Luc Godard

Back on the road

Congratulations! You have made it through the creative connections boot camp. Perhaps you have already noticed a difference: You're seeing more connections in your everyday life. You have an easier time generating ideas. New connections hit you unprompted.

Each time people complete the boot camp, we notice the same thing: They generate more ideas, they create more original solutions, and they work with more confidence.

One sunny afternoon, after Dorte had been running the Creative Communications department for a few years, she was talking in the park with the same creative director who had initially discouraged her from teaching creativity. He was still in advertising, and he was still skeptical: "I don't believe you can teach people to be creative."

"I don't do it by teaching them to do ads," she replied. "I don't even do it by teaching them to do creative problem solving. I focus on connection making. I pull that one skill out of the creative process and train it over and over. And when they go back to the process, they are so much better at creative problem solving, because they have trained the muscle that helps them do it."

It boils down to one thing, she said: "Highly creative people are good at seeing connections. By enhancing your ability to see connections, you can enhance your creativity."

He thought it over. "That I can believe," he said.

Teaching creativity is a lot like teaching music theory. It doesn't make you musical, but it makes you a better musician. By learning creative thinking skills and by practicing the essential skill of seeing connections, you have enhanced your innate creativity. You can face any challenge that needs creative thinking and do the job better.

The Portfolio Recommendation Ride
Chauffeurs: Stefan Arnoldus and Jacob Norremark

Driving into the future

Before we give you our parting gifts of tools, here's a send off story to give you confidence that connection making can impact your life, especially at its crucial moments.

At the end of their three-year program in creative communications, Jacob and Stefan, two talented students in Dorte's graduating class needed to get a job. Not just any job. They were looking for a world-class position in advertising. They wanted to work with top talent. They wanted big opportunities. In big firms. In big cities. And they wanted to stay together as a creative team. They needed to make high-level connections that were political, strategic, and financially rewarding.

So they hatched a plan. A few months before graduation, they decided to go to Cannes Lions, the International Festival of Creativity, in France. It would be the perfect place to meet advertising executives from Google, Ogilvy and Saatchi & Saatchi and other high-flying agencies, who would be there for the festival. If only they could find a way to get job interviews with these ad execs.

So they started to connect the dots. They diverged on all the things that ad executives coming to Cannes might need, and they suddenly saw a simple, brilliant connection: a ride. All these executives would need a ride from the airport to the festival. So Jacob and Stefan invented the Portfolio Recommendation Ride. They bought two white chauffeur uniforms and rented the most expensive car they could afford. For a week, they drove executives from the airport to the Festival in exchange for a twenty-minute interview and the chance to show off their advertising portfolio en route.

They got riders. They got international press. And of course, they got a stack of job opportunities.

"You can't use up creativity. The more you use the more you have."

Maya Angelou

Send off

Does this "seeing connections" thing really work? It does. We wouldn't have committed all this to paper if the combined evidence from the classroom, the ivory tower, and the neuroscience labs had not been utterly convincing.

Daily discoveries about the plasticity of the brain are an invitation to all of us to cultivate a better brain. Thanks to the time and effort you've devoted to the art of making connections, you are bound to perform better and be more at ease the next time you have to generate ideas or go into a brainstorming sessions. But the real payoff is in cultivating an ability to see beyond what's there, to generate the third option, to play with more cards than you have in your hand. The real value is the ability is to see, not just what's given, but what's possible.

In the final chapter, we leave you with tools that will help you along.

We wish you well on you journey of discovery.

Dorte Nielsen & Sarah Thurber

Pen by Karina Tørnsø Johannessen

Creative connection tools

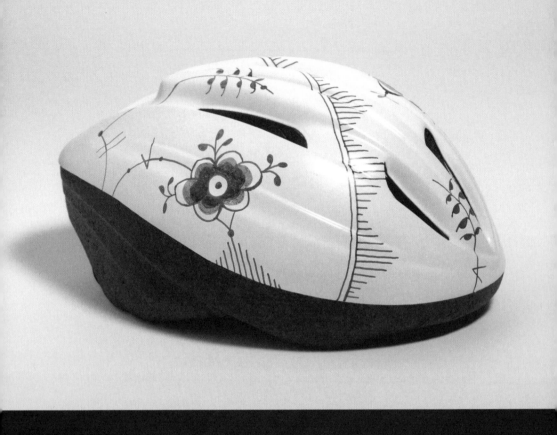

Porcelain Helmet by Mette Nyhus Skammeritz.
Shark Tooth Knife by Thomas Jorgensen Parastatidis.

Creative connections tools

You're ready to take your connection-making abilities on the road. Our parting gift is a set of three tools to take along. Tools are meant to make a job easier. We've picked some tools that are particularly good at the job of connection making. They work the way your brain works. They are excerpted from *Idébogen [The Idea Book]* by Dorte Nielsen, and printed here with permission. Pull them out when you need to think creatively.

    1. Mind Mapping
    2. Cross Connections
    3. Random Inspiration

In the next pages, we'll describe each tool in detail. The explanations may seem a bit elaborate. The first time you try them out, they might feel a bit forced. But keep at it. Once you get the hang of working with these tools, they'll feel like an extension of your brain, and it will all come naturally to you.

Tool 1: Mind mapping

Mind mapping is a tool that helps you focus on connections. You can use mind mapping for organizing information, or you can use it to generate new ideas and connections. A mind map looks like a visual web of connections. It lets you reach further into the corners of a subject and create a good overview.

In school, we learned to think linearly. We write things down in columns and rows. Linear thinking shows up in our daily doings as shopping lists and ledgers.

Straight lists have their advantages, but when you want to create new ideas, it's important to break with the limits of linear thinking and think outside rows and frames. A mind map can help you do that.

Tony Buzan, the originator of mind mapping, believed that writing down information this way was a better reflection of how the brain actually works: not in straight lines but in organic, branching structures, with patterns and associations.

The key to understanding a mind map is to appreciate its structure. Unlike a list that starts at the top and works down, a mind map starts in the middle and works out. At the center is the kernel, the central theme, subject, or challenge. From there, information, thoughts, and ideas radiate out in all directions, taking the form of words, pictures, or symbols. A mind map's structure is almost like seeing a tree from the top: It's a trunk surrounded by limbs, branches, twigs, and leaves.

Multiple uses

A mind map lets you keep the big picture in mind and work in many directions, elaborating on many elements at the same time, thereby increasing the possibility of seeing new connections. It's therefore a great tool to use at the start of a creative process.

You can also use it when you're stuck. A mind map can be a perfect place to do a "braindump." Start with the problem in the middle and unload, bit by bit, all thought and ideas, including the confusing, interrelated pieces that are swirling around in your head. The mind map you make often helps you see things more clearly.

When you're brainstorming, a mind map can be a great way to record your branching thoughts. Capture your divergent ideas as they arise. It will help to empty your brain and clear room for new thinking.

Mind maps also serve as a way to record notes, organize and reorganize thoughts, and consciously create new combinations, associations, and ideas. Keep your mind map nearby. You may find yourself referring to it again and again through your work process.

SPORT

TENNIS

BASKETBALL

FOOTBALL

BADMINTON

RUGBY

HOCKEY

CYCLING

SKIING

GOLF

Here are examples of two ways to generate some initial thoughts for a sports poster. On this page, you see a linear list. On the next page, you see a mind map. You can see how the mind map lends itself naturally to divergent exploration and connection making, whereas the list keeps you on one train of thought.

MMING

GOLF

BASKETBALL

FOOTBALL

AL !!!

MINTON

TENNIS —

SH

RACING

SPEEDWAY

LING

ART

CHAMPAGNE

VICTORY

TEARS

WIN

LOSE

HOCKEY

GAME

SPORT

DRESSING ROOM

FITNESS

MOVEMENT

SWEATBAND

PILLS

DOPING

MONEY

ATHLETICS

OLYMP FLAM

OLYMPICS

CHAMPIONSHIP

COMPETITION

REFEREE —

STADIUM

SPECTATOR

SWEAT

SMELLY SOCKS

FOOTBALL BOOT

SPORTS BAG

BALLET SHOES

SKATES

Make a mind map

1. Start with a large piece of paper.

2. Draw an oval in the center in which you write your challenge.

3. Start to record the ideas that stem from your challenge. Start in the middle, and let your thoughts literally branch out from there. Everything is allowed: words, drawings, pictures, and symbols.

4. Let new themes, subjects, and ideas arise. Let your thoughts run freely.

5. The good thing about a mindmap is that you can work in many directions at once. If you can't find more associations to your main theme, move on to another word in your mindmap and connect to that. Add another word. And another. There is always a path forward, so your thinking well won't run dry.

6. Let your fantasy rule. Make loads of visual ideas, write down things that are concrete, e.g. visual ideas, symbols, and metaphors. Remember to enjoy yourself.

7. Let your mindmap help you to make "creative leaps" between branches and find connections between things that previously had nothing to do with each other.

8. Keep on until you reach the edge of the paper, pushing outward so that your thoughts no longer directly associate with the theme in the middle. It's often here that original and unexpected ideas emerge.

9. Check to see that your mind map covers all the important points. Fill in any gaps. The better your mind map, the more it will serve you as a launch pad for ideas.

Tool 2: Cross Connections

For years, artists and inventors have been busy combining things that previously had nothing to do with each other in order to create something new. When it works, the impact is stunning: so original, yet so simple.

Highly creative people seem to do this naturally, but is there a way to do it deliberately?

The Cross Connections tool is an easy way to combine unrelated objects into something new. This tool will help you generate a lot of ideas very quickly. Not all of them will be useful. A number might be absurd. But don't let that stop you. The more ideas you produce, the greater the chances of you creating one good idea. As two-time Nobel prize-winner Linus Pauling said, "The best way to have a good idea is to have a lot of ideas."

The Cross Connections tool is based on visual combinations, and it's particularly useful for communicating one idea with multiple examples, or for communicating two topics at once through a combination.

Narrow your subject and choose two themes that illuminate it from very different angles. For example, the subject "revolution" might be divided into the themes "people" and "uprising." The greater the contrast between the themes the better. More contrast leads to more interesting ideas.

Make cross connections

1. Start with a clearly defined challenge.

2. Choose two themes that illustrate or represent your challenge.

3. Create a column for each theme. Fill each column with a list of simple nouns, which reflect different aspects of the theme. Choose nouns that can be depicted as visual symbols, icons, and line drawings. (Finding good visual items can be a challenge. You can identify nouns by looking through the information you've gathered on the topic or by creating a mind map centered around each theme.)

Theme 1:   Theme 2:

_____   _____

_____   _____

_____   _____

_____   _____

_____   _____

_____   _____

4. Look at the two columns and begin to combine items. Take a pictorial idea from one column and freely combine it with one from the other column. This should give you some simple strong visual ideas that communicate the two themes.

5. Once you've made the most obvious combinations, the ones that first took your fancy, you get down to the fun part of the work. Close your eyes. Draw lines between the two columns so your lines connect the two lists in a random way. Sketch these combinations, no matter how crazy they seem. It is worth spending time on each combination. What may seem an impossible combination in the beginning can end up as a great idea. Here's where you'll get some unexpected solutions that only appear if you allow chance to rule. This step produces many strange solutions including some you cannot possibly use. Have fun with it, laugh, and use the useless ideas as springboards to new original ones.

6. Generate as many ideas as you possibly can. If you started out with six pictorial ideas in each theme, you should now have at least thirty-six different solution (6x6). It is often worth making several solutions for each combination, since there are many ways to visually combine, for example, a flip flop with running spikes. Remember not to judge along the way, as that can hold you back from producing some of the best solutions. Generate your ideas first and evaluate them later.

7. Review the combinations you have made. Do any of them inspire more new ideas? Is there anything you have overlooked? If an extra idea is hiding somewhere, now is the time to capture it.

8. Then converge. Evaluate, judge, and choose your idea.

An example of how to make Cross Connections. The challenge was to create a poster for a sporting holiday.

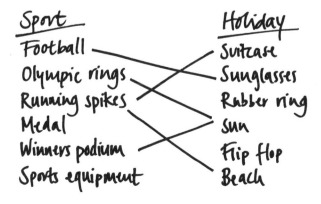

Cross-connected thoughts and ideas created for a poster with the two themes sport and holiday.

Fruit Jar Holder.

45265 Fruit-Jar Holder, for holding jar while hot or when taking off caps.
For 1 quart jars, each........ ....$0.15
Per dozen.. 1.65
45266 For 2 quart jars, each. .$0.17
Per dozen... 1.85
For price of fruit jars, see Grocery List.

Plate Lifter.

45267 Triumph Plate Lifter, for lifting hot plates from oven.
Each...... ....$0.13

Pot Cleaners.

Pot Cleaner or Wire Dish Cloth, the most convenient and popular utensil extant: pots and kettles can be cleaned of grease easily, and when done there is no dirty dish rag to wash out.   Each. Per doz
45268 Pot Cleaner, round wire, small.....$0.05 $0.54
45269 Pot Cleaner, round wire, large..... .07 .75

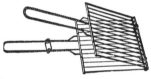

45270 Handled Pot Cleaner, tinned wire handle, bright wire rings; total length, 9½ inches.
Each .... $0.08 Per dozen $0.85

Broilers or Toasters—Retinned.

45275—
Long.	Wide.		No. bars.	Each.
9 x	6......	....	9....	$0.12
9 x	7½..........................		11....	.14
9 x	9..........................		11....	.15
9 x	10½..........		15....	.16
9 x	12..........................		17 ..	.18
9 x	13½..........		19	.20

Vegetable Boilers.

45278 Made of wire. Can also be used for boiling eggs.
Size	6 in.	7 in.	8 in.	9 in.
Each	14c.	17c.	19c.	21c.

Corn Popper.

45280 Corn Poppers, tin top. 1 quart. Each....$0.08
Per dozen............................. ... .87
45281 Corn Poppers, wire top, 2 quarts.
Each............ .... .15
Per dozen........................... 1.62
45282 Corn Poppers, 4 quarts, each............. .75
45283 "   "   " 8   "   "............. 2.75
The 4 and 8 quart poppers are such used by confectioners, street venders, etc.

⌇ Wire Toasters.

Potato Masher.

45292 Tinned wire Potato Masher, wood handle.
Each. Per doz.
Large......... ....$0.09 $0.90

Fly Traps.

45295 The Champion Fly Trap, made of fine wire cloth; a very strong and well made trap, with a high cone; will catch flies faster than any other.
Each........ ....$0.15
Per doz 1.62

Dish Covers.

45296 Round Dish Covers, made of blued wire cloth.
Size.....	6	7	8	9	10
Each	$0.04	$0.05	$0.06	$0.07	$0.09
Per doz.	.40	.50	.60	.70	.90

45297 Round Dish Covers, made of blued wire cloth, in sets of 5, one of each size, 6, 7, 8, 9, 10.
Per set..... ....$0.28

Bird Cages.

45300 Bird Cage, round, all brass, 8½ inches in diameter, with seed cups, perch, etc.; has bell bottom.
Each....................$1 00

45305 Squirrel Cages, for red or chip squirrels, made of wire, japanned; size, over all, 18 in. long; 10 in. wide, 13 in. high; size of body, 10 in. long, 9 in. wide, 12 in. high; size of wheel, 6½ in. long, 9 in. in diameter.
Price, each............$1.60

Climax Rat Trap.

45306 A Self-Setting Rat Catcher. Convenient bait box, novel tilting platform. This trap is made with a bait box that is supplied through a lid at the top. It holds the bait alluringly to the rat, yet he cannot readily withdraw it through the fine meshes. The trap is made of heavy double crimped steel wires which cannot be displaced or broken. The trap will maintain its original shape and can be shipped compactly and will always reach destination in good condition. Size of trap, 20 inches long, 8 inches wide, 7 inches high. Price, each................$1.00
Per dozen................................... 10.50

Combination Rat and Mouse Trap.

45307 This is made of retinned wire cloth and may be used to catch either mice or rats. When set for mice, the end is closed, the mice entering at the hole inside the trap: small wire door drops behind them that can be easily opened by the mice on the outside but not from inside; as one mouse will act as a decoy for another, quite a number may be caught at once. When rats are to be caught it is set as seen in cut. Weight, 1 lb. 13 oz. Each $0.35

Tool 3: Random inspiration

Random inspiration is a classic tool to drum up new and unexpected ideas. Followers of Edward de Bono, author of *Six Thinking Hats* and *Lateral Thinking*, will know this tool as "Random Input" or "Random word." Disciples of Sid Parnes and creative problem solving will know it as "Forced Connections."

This tool asks you to put together unlike objects and make connections in places you would not normally think to look. While anything can be a source of inspiration, this tool demands that you pick an object found purely by chance. Let chance rule! Let the unforeseen connection challenge you to see your problem in a new way.

Choosing the items can be a fun task in itself. You can use words, pictures, objects, anything! Scan your surroundings to find new sources of inspiration and avoid all your usual sources.

- Close your eyes and point to a word in the dictionary.

- Find a picture deck and pick a card.

- Choose a word from the "magnet poetry" on your refrigerator.

- Open a catalog at random; choose the third thing in the second column.

- Find a book, magazine, newspaper or whatever and choose the seventh noun on page 27.

- Turn your TV on and choose the fifth word said by the hero.

- Visit your neighbor and choose the first piece of furniture you see.

- The possibilities are endless.

Using random inspiration

Before you use this "Random Inspiration" tool to inspire ideas, be sure you have a clearly defined problem.

1. Frame your problem as an open-ended question

"How might I ...?"

2. Choose something at random

Remember, the key to this method is to let yourself be inspired, stimulated, or provoked by random input in order to avoid your usual solutions. (The more surprising and unexpected the item, the better. If your item is too close to the problem, it will not spur new thinking.)

3. Solve your problem using the randomly chosen item

Find a link between the random item and your problem. What do these two things have in common? How can they be related to each other? How can the item or its attributes suggest a solution to your problem? Take your time. Focus your thoughts. Let the random object stimulate your fantasy. Create connections. Ask questions. Let the item prompt you to see your problem in a new light. Be serious. Be flippant. Be rational. Then be irrational.

to we dirt flower speak pod er co co of above day know secret red

the would was will we cup kiss is magic

up heal s to at vas her when from miss sister cak ce

question must be haunt has she and seep ize

each ed er ed lip about star coffee ful sno too over tot you ing red

worry was and sky warm use my job he er circle

ice ed hy prisoner are ing always hot for breath

porcelain boy every slow bone fever like put one concrete ghost have morning make naked

did bring is wild tion award soon es it ing melt let dog ing you did web s

slucent for but learn girl never delicious live it him his see pierce they daz aps or

References

Adobe. (2014). *Seeking Creative Candidates: Hiring for the Future*. Adobe Systems. http://wwwimages.adobe.com/content/dam/Adobe/en/education/pdfs/creative-candidates-study-0914.pdf

Bachman, R. (2011, February 28). Nike's Holy Grail: Bowerman Family Unearths Long-lost Waffle Iron. *The Oregonian*. Retrieved from: http://blog.oregonlive.com/behindducksbeat/2011/02/nikes_holy_grail_bowerman_fami.html.

Backman, M. E., & Tuckman, B. W. (1972). Review: Remote Associates Test. *Journal of Educational Measurement*, 9(2), 161-162.

Baird, L. L. (1972). Review of the Remote Associates Test. In O. K. Buros (Ed.), *Seventh Mental Measurements Yearbook*, (vol. 7). Highland Park, NJ: Buros Institute of Mental Measurements.

Benyus, J. M. (2002). *Biomimicry: Innovation Inspired by Nature*. New York: Harper Perennial. http://biomimicry.org/

Bloom, B. S., Englehart, M. D., Furst, E. J., Hill, W. H., & Krathwohl, D. R. (Eds.). (1956). *Taxonomy of Educational Objectives: The Classification of Educational Goals. Handbook 1: Cognitive Domain*. New York, NY: David McKay.

Brassai, G., (1999). *Conversations with Picasso*. Chicago, IL: The University of Chicago Press.

Cabra, J. F. (2009). *Definitions and Theories of Creativity*. Unpublished Presentation, The International Center for Studies in Creativity, State University of New York, Buffalo, New York.

Colvin, G. (2010). *Talent is Overrated*. New York, NY: Penguin.

Davis, G. A. (2004). *Creativity is Forever*. Dubuque, IA: Kendall/Hunt.

Dietrich, A. (2004). The Cognitive Neuroscience of Creativity. *Psychonomic Bulletin & Review*, 11(6), 1011-1026.

Dietrich, A. (2007). Who's Afraid of a Cognitive Neuroscience of Creativity? *Methods*, 42, 22-27.

Fink, A., Grabner, R. H., Benedek, M., Staudt, B., Neubauer, A. C. (2006). Divergent Thinking Training is Related to Frontal Electroencephalogram Alpha Synchronization. *European Journal of Neuroscience*, 23, 2241-2246.

Fink, A., Benedek, M., Grabner, R. H., Staudt, B., & Neubauer, A. C. (2007). Creativity Meets Neuroscience: Experimental Tasks for the Neuroscientific Study of Creative Thinking. *Methods*, 42, 68-76.

Fink, A., Grabner, R. H., Benedek, M., Reishofer,G., Hauswirth, V., Fally, M., Neuper, C., Ebner, F., Neubauer, A. C. (2009a). The Creative Brain: Investigation of Brain Activity During Creative Problem Solving by Means of EEG and fMRI. *Human Brain Mapping*, 30, 734-748.

Fink, A., Graif, B., Neubauer, A. C. (2009b). Brain Correlates Underlying Creative Thinking: EEG Alpha Activity in Professional vs. Novice Dancers. *NeuroImage*, 46, 854-862.

Fink, A., Grabner, R.H., Gebauer, D., Reishofer, G., Koschutnig, K., Ebner, F. (2010). Enhancing Creativity by Means of Cognitive Stimulation: Evidence from an fMRI Study. *NeuroImage*, 52, 1687-1695.

Fink, A. (2011). fMRI/EEG. Abstracts of SAN Meeting / *Neuroscience Letters* 500S, e1-e54, p. e15.

Firestien, R. L. (1996). *Leading on the Creative Edge: Gaining Competitive Advantage Through the Power of Creative Problem Solving*. Colorado Springs, CO: Pinon Press.

Frey, C. B., Osborne, M. A., (2013, September 17). *The Future of Employment: How Susceptible are Jobs to Computerization?* Oxford University Programme on the Impacts of Future Technology. http://www.oxfordmartin.ox.ac.uk/downloads/academic/The_Future_of_Employment.pdf

Gardner, H. (1983). *Frames of Mind: The Theory of Multiple Intelligences*. New York, NY: Basic.

Gordon, W. J. J. (1961). *Synectics*. New York, NY: Harper & Row.

Gordon, W. J. J. & Poze, T. (1971). *The Basic Course in Synectics* (Vol 1-6). Cambrigde, MA: Porpoise Books.

Guilford, J. P. (1977). *Way Beyond the IQ: Guide to Improving Intelligence and Creativity*. Buffalo, NY: Creative Education Foundation.

Hadamard, J. (1945). *The Mathematician's Mind*. Princeton, NJ: Princeton University Press.

Hurson, T. (2008). *Think Better: An Innovator's Guide to Productive Thinking*. New York, NY: Mc Graw Hill.

IBM (2010). *Capitalising on Complexity: Insights from the Global Chief Executive Officer Study*. Portsmouth, UK: IBM Institute for Business Value.

Jarosz, A. F., Colflesh, G. J. H., & Wiley, J. (2012). Uncorking the Muse: Alcohol Intoxication Facilitates Creative Problem Solving. *Consciousness and Cognition*, Vol. 21, Issue 1, 487-493.

Jones, D. (2012). *Everyday Creativity (Powerful Creativity Techniques to Be Used on All Your Everyday Challenges)*. Multimedia CD. Star Thrower.

Kaufman, A. B., Kornilov, S. A., Bristol, A. S., Tan, M., & Grigorenko, E. L. (2010). The Neurobiological Foundation of Creative Cognition. In J. C. Kaufman & R. J. Sternberg (Eds.) *The Cambridge Handbook of Creativity* (pp. 216-232). New York, NY: Cambridge University Press.

Kaufman, J. C., & Sternberg, R. J. (Eds.). (2010). *The Cambridge Handbook of Creativity*. New York, NY: Cambridge University Press.

Kirton, M. J. (1994). *Adaptors and Innovators: Styles of Creativity and Problem Solving* (Rev. ed.). London, England: Routledge.

Koestler, A. (1964). *The Act of Creation*. New York, NY: Macmillan.

Kringelbach, M.L. & Cattrell, A. (2015). An Architecture of Pleasure and Pain. Combining Art and Science to Make Sense of the Brain. *LA Plus*, 2:10-17.

Kringelbach, M.L. & Phillips, H. (2014). *Emotion: Pleasure and Pain in the Brain*. Oxford: Oxford Univesity Press.

Martindale, C. (1999). Biological basis of creativity. In R. J. Sternberg (Ed.), *Handbook of Creativity* (pp. 137-152). Cambrigde, UK: Cambridge University Press.

Mednick, S. A. (1962). The Associative Basis of the Creative Process. *Psychological Review*, 69(3), 220-232.

Mednick, M. T., & Mednick, S. A. (1967). *Examiner's Manual. Remote Associates Test. College and Adult Forms 1 and 2*. University of Michigan. Boston, MA: Houghton Mifflin Company.

Michalko, M. (1991). *Thinkerstoys: A Handbook of Business Creativity for the 90s*. Berkeley, CA: Ten Speed Press.

Miller, B., Vehar, J., Firestien, R., Thurber, S., & Nielsen, D. (2011). *Creativity Unbound: An Introduction to Creative Process* (5th ed.). Evanston, IL: FourSight.

Miller, E. K., & Cohen, J. D. (2001). An Integrative Theory of Prefrontal Cortex Function. *Annu. Rev. Neurosci.* 24, 167-202.

Nielsen, D. (2001). *Idébogen: Kreative Værktøjer og Metoder til Idé- og Konceptudvikling. [The Idea Book: Creative Tools and Techniques for Idea and Concept Development]*. Copenhagen, Denmark: Grafisk Litteratur.

Nielsen, D., & Hartmann, K. (2005). *Inspired: How Creative People Think, Work and Find Inspiration*. Amsterdam, The Netherlands: BIS Publishers.

Nielsen, D., Kej., T., & Granholm, K. (2009). *Grundbog for Art Directors: Regler du kan bruge eller bryde. [Art Director's ABC. Rules to Use or Break]*. Copenhagen, Denmark: Grafisk Litteratur.

Osborn, A. (1963). *Applied Imagination* (3rd ed.). New York, NY: Charles Scribner's Sons.

Parnes, S. J. (Ed.). (1992). Synectics—Making and Breaking Connections. [Editor's note on the paper "On being explicit about creative process" by W. J. J. Gordon.] *Sourcebook for Creative Problem Solving*. (pp. 164-165). Hadley, MA: Creative Education.

Poincaré, H. (1913). *The Foundation of Science*. Lancaster, PA: Science Press.

Prince, G. M. (1992). The Mindspring Theory: A New Development from Synectics Research. In S.J. Parnes (Ed.) *Source Book for Creative Problem Solving*. (pp. 177-193). Buffalo, NY: Creative Education Foundation Press.

Puccio, G. J., Burnett, C. B., Acar, S., Yudess, J., Cabra, J. F., & Hollinger, M. (work in progress). Creative Problem Solving in Small Groups: The Effects of *Training on Idea Generation, Creativity of Solutions, and Leadership Effectiveness.* The International Center for Studies in Creativity, Buffalo State.

Puccio, G. J., Cabra, J. F., & Schwagler, N. (in progress). *Creativity and Innovation in Organizations: A Personal Guide for 21st Century Innovators* (working title). Thousand Oaks, CA: Sage Publications.

Puccio, G., Mance, M., & Murdock, M. (2011). *Creative Leadership: Skills that Drive Change* (2nd ed.). Thousand Oaks, California: Sage Publications.

Rae, N. *The Art of Observation: Elliott Erwitt.* http://fadedandblurred.com/spotlight/elliott-erwitt/

Rose, L. H., & Lin, H. T. (1984). A Meta-Analysis of Long-Term Creativity Training Programs. *The Journal of Creative Behavior,* 18, 11-22.

Sawyer, K. (2011). The Cognitive Neuroscience of Creativity: A Critical Review, *Creativity Research Journal,* 23(2), 137-154.

Scott, G. M., Leritz, L. E., & Mumford, M. D. (2004). The Effectiveness of Creativity Training: A Meta-Analysis. *Creativity Research Journal,* 16, 361-388.

Stross, R. E. (2008). *The Wizard of Menlo Park: How Thomas Alva Edison Invented the Modern World.* New York: Three Rivers Press.

Sternberg, R. J. (1985). *Beyond IQ: A Triarchic Theory of Human Intelligence.* New York: Cambridge University Press.

Taylor, C. W. (1986). Cultivating Simultaneous Student Growth in both Multiple Creative Talents and Knowledge. In J. S. Renzulli (Ed.) *Systems and Models for Developing Programs for the Gifted and Talented* (pp. 307-350). Mansfield, CT: Creative Learning Press.

Torrance, E. P. (1972). Can We Teach Children to Think Creatively? *The Journal of Creative Behavior,* 6, 114-143.

Torrance, E. P. (2004). Predicting the Creativity of Elementary School Children (1958-80) — and The Teacher Who 'Made a Difference.' In D. J. Treffinger (Ed.), *Creativity and Giftedness* (pp. 35-49). Thousand Oaks, CA: Corwin Press.

Vincent, P. H., Decker, B. P., & Mumford, M. D. (2002). Divergent Thinking, Intelligence, and Expertise: A Test of Alternative Models. *Creativity Research Journal,* 14, 163-178.

Young, J. W. (1975). *A Technique for Producing Ideas.* Chicago, IL: NTC Business Books.

Zollo, P. (2003). *Songwriters on Songwriting.* 4th expanded edition. Cincinnati, OH: De Capo Press.

Anger Management by Lil'Ol'Lady

Credits

Page 14. *Lampella* by Neela Menik Wedage, student work.

Page 16. A close up shot of a waffle iron, Kitch Bain, Shutterstock.com.
Nike Waffle Trainer: J. Crew's Nike® Vintage Collection Waffle® Racer Sneakers. Lyst.com

Page 19. *Candle* by Dorte N ielsen.

Page 20-21. *Spoons* by Tammes Bernstein, student work.

Page 24. *Lightbulb* by Trine Quistgaard, student work.

Page 26. *Twist Cone* by Mads Schmidt, student work.

Page 28. *Christmas Tree* by Mikkel Møller.

Page 30-31. *Bull* by Picasso. Photograph by Gjon Mili. Getty Images.

Page 32. *Managua, Nicaragua* by Elliott Erwitt.

Page 37. Close-up shot of Burdock seeds, Julie Lucht, Shutterstock.com

Page 38. Above: Kingfisher. Photograph by Michael L. Blaird. Creative Commons.

Page 38. Below: Bullettrain. Photograph from gus2travel.com. Creative Commons.

Page 42. *Tie* by Maria Birkholm Marcher, student work.

Page 46. Above: Leaves. Original source unknown.

Page 46. Below: *Pringels*. Photograph by Isabel Smart and Dorte Nielsen.

Page 52. *Brain Freeze* by Jennifer Tonndorff, student work. Photograph by Louis Gretlund.

Page 57. *The Problem Solver* by Mark Rif Torbensen, Mathias Birkvad and Kristoffer Gandsager, CP+B Copenhagen.

Page 58. *Librarian*. Concept by Dorte Nielsen. Illustration by Andrew Smart.

Page 59. *Conductor*. Concept by Dorte Nielsen. Illustration by Andrew Smart.

Page 61. *Your Inner Librarian*. Concept by Dorte Nielsen. Illustration by Andrew Smart.

Page 62. *Birdhouse* by Andreas Green Lorentzen, student work.

Page 64. Reference: Puccio, G., Mance, M., & Murdock, M. (2011). *Creative Leadership: Skills that Drive Change* (2nd ed.). Illustration by Dorte Nielsen.

Page 67. *Shower and Funnel*. Concept by Dorte Nielsen. Illustration by Andrew Smart.

Page 68. Reference: Puccio, G., Mance, M., & Murdock, M. (2011). *Creative Leadership: Skills that Drive Change* (2nd ed.). Illustration by Dorte Nielsen.

Page 70. *Guidelines Divergent Thinking*. Reference: Puccio, G., Mance, M., & Murdock, M. (2011). *Creative Leadership: Skills that Drive Change* (2nd ed.). Thousand Oaks, California: Sage Publications. Illustration by Dorte Nielsen.

Page 71. *Guidelines Convergent Thinking.* Reference: Puccio, G., Mance, M., & Murdock, M. (2011). *Creative Leadership: Skills that Drive Change* (2nd ed.). Thousand Oaks, California: Sage Publications. Illustration by Dorte Nielsen.

Page 72. *Sparkling Idea* by Sofie Engelbrecht Simonsen, student work.

Page 76. *Carrot.* Photograph by Dorte Nielsen.

Page 80. Pretest and posttest from the 1001 ideas course taught by Dorte Nielsen.

Page 81. Self assessment from the 1001 ideas course taught by Dorte Nielsen.

Page 84. *Pacman* by Miller Møller.

Page 86. *Winter Observation.* Photograph by Dorte Nielsen.

Page 89. *Horse* by Louise Arve, student work.

Page 90. *Extra Pair of Hands* by Simone Wärme, student work. Model: Klara Vilshammer Christiansen.

Page 92-93. *Tool* by Sebastian Risom Drejer, student work.

Page 94. Christmas card by Mikkel Møller.

Page 98. Main image: *Rainwater Device* by August Laustsen, student work.

Page 98. Small image: Rainwater Collector. Source unknown.

Page 101. Above: *Kitchen Light* by Kasper Dohlmann, student work.

Page 101. Below: *Ballet Dancer* by Line Schou, student work.

Page 102. *Dangerous Idea* by Jeppe Vidstrup Nielsen, student work.

Page 106-149. The copyright on the individual exercises is held by Dorte Nielsen.

Page 106. Above: *Coffin* by Sune Overby Sørensen, student work. Photography source unknown.

Page 106. Below: *Running Shoes* by Camilla Berlick, student work.

Page 109. *Bull* by Picasso. Photograph by Gjon Mili. Getty Images.

Page 110-111. *Bike parts.* Concept by Dorte Nielsen. Illustrations by Andrew Smart.

Page 112-113. *Visual Connections.* Concept by Dorte Nielsen. Illustrations by Andrew Smart.

Page 118. Above: *Woodpecker* by Lea Brisell, student work.

Page 118. Below: *Tandem Slippers* by Camilla Søholt Larsen, student work.

Page 121. Photograph 1: *Crime Scene* by [puamelia] - Crime scene do not cross / @CSI?cafe (CC BY-SA 2.0). Photograph 2-5 by Dorte Nielsen.

Page 125. *Random Visuals.* Concept by Dorte Nielsen. Illustrations by Andrew Smart.

Page 126. Above: *Lego Shoes* by Jesper Wendelbo Lindeløv, student work.

Page 126. Below: *All Terrain Shoes* by René Schultz, student work. Photography source unknown.

Page 128. *Random Words.* Concept by Dorte Nielsen. Photograph by Sarah Thurber.

Page 129. Nine photographs by Dorte Nielsen.

Page 130. *Candle variations.* Concept by Dorte Nielsen. Illustrations by Andrew Smart.

Acknowledgments

Putting this book together has been such a joy. Not to say that it wasn't a ton of work. Quite the contrary, it was an epic wrestling match with the creative process: Sometimes, we had it by the collar; other times, we were bumping around in the dark. But as a creative team, we both entered this challenge with an understanding of the science of creativity and equipped with great tools for collaboration, communication, and idea generation. And we used them all.

Of course, there are people who made this book possible: our husbands, children, mentors, editors, publishers, and students. First, we are eternally grateful to our husbands, Andrew Smart and Blair Miller. They had unflagging confidence in our ability to pull this off and tolerated years of late night and early morning Skype calls from trains, planes, and kitchen counters. They read and reread multiple versions. In the end, they kept the rest of our lives from devolving into untended chaos. We thank our wonderful parents and fabulous children, Cole, Thomas, Becca and two Isabels (we both have one). They have all been loyal cheerleaders, quietly shouldering the extra burdens of laundry, lunch making, and carpool planning that book writing seems to require of authors' families.

We thank our mentor Dr. Gerard Puccio, director of the International Center for Studies in Creativity. His thought leadership in the movement to ignite creative literacy around the world and his graduate program, where we first began our collaboration, has profoundly shaped the way we understand and teach creativity.

If you knew all the work they did, you, too would be deeply appreciative of Tim Hurson, Ellisa Goldsmith, and Katrine Granholm, our early readers, who were able to offer sage advice when we were too close to the work to see it clearly. Not to mention, Andrew Smart, who went way beyond the call of spousal duty to pen the dozens of stellar illustrations that appear throughout this book.

Our thanks to BIS Publishers, both to Rudolf Van Wezel, who immediately saw the potential of this work and to Bionda Diaz, who made it a reality.

Thanks also to the Danish School of Media and Journalism and the hundreds of students at Creative Communications, who over the last decade, have been extremely open minded, experimenting endlessly in the quest to find the perfect mix of exercises to enhance their innate creativity and build on their natural creative talents.

A special thanks to the students who gave us permission to publish their images in this book, and to model maker Joachim Weilland, who year after year, has helped students realize their ideas and build their inventions. Hats off to Mikkel Møller for his ceaseless search for new connections and for giving us permission to show a few of his best in this book.

Deep gratitude for Dorte's colleagues at Creative Communications, Katrine Granholm, Ulrik Jessen, Clare McNally, Henrik Birkvig, and Cathrina Ferreira.

We thank Morten Kringelbach for an inspiring train ride, the FourSight team for their patience and support, the faculty of the ICSC graduate program, and our creativity colleagues around the world for their commitment to nurturing creativity in others.

Thinking back, if it hadn't been for the CREA conference in Italy, the two of us never would have met at the Villa Balbi Hotel, where, during our very first real conversation together, we knew we had made a brilliant connection.

Nielsen and Thurber both completed their Masters of Science in Creativity at the International Center for Studies in Creativity, New York, where they were jointly awarded the Firestien Family Creative Achievement Award for developing a visual model of creative process that has since been adopted by schools, Fortune 500 companies, and nonprofits around the world. For more information, visit www.see-connections.com.

About the authors

Dorte Nielsen

Nielsen's parents, both chemical engineers, were mildly alarmed when she launched a career in creativity. After working as an art director at Ogilvy in London and winning advertising awards at D&AD and Cannes among others, she returned home to Copenhagen and founded the Creative Communications department, now part of the Danish School of Media and Journalism. Today, her creativity curriculum has helped make Creative Communications one of the most the most award-winning bachelors program in advertising in the world. After more than a decade training aspiring creative directors, Nielsen took her uniquely effective creativity curriculum to primary schools. Now a keynoter, educator, and the author of "The Idea Book" and "Inspired," she is exploring the neuroscience of creativity, while serving her second term as Chairman of Creative Circle, the Danish society for the creative industries. She continues to dedicate her career to nurturing the creative talents of others.

Sarah Thurber

Thurber showed wayward signs of creative thinking early on with the creation of a 6-foot paper mache alligator in her parents' basement. An early career as a freelance writer took her around the world, landing her eventually in Chicago where her writing began to focus exclusively on the topic of creativity. She edited "Creativity Unbound" which has been used as a text in colleges and universities around the globe. Thurber is now managing partner of FourSight, an international innovation company that publishes the FourSight Thinking Profile and supports research on cognitive diversity and collaborative problem solving. Today she is an author, keynoter, product designer and thought leader in creative thinking styles. Having witnessed the positive impact that deliberate creativity has had on her family, marriage, neighborhood, schools, business, and clients, she is determined to share these insights with others.

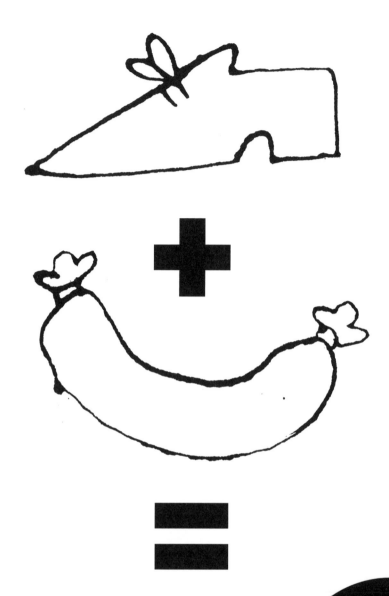

Creative Thinker's Exercise Book

A workbook with more exercises and connection-making activities to enhance your creativity.

Coming out fall 2016

**For more visit the site
www.see-connections.com**